A Guide to the Mental Health Act 1983

Robert Bluglass
MD FRCPsych DPM
Professor of Forensic Psychiatry,
University of Birmingham
Consultant Forensic Psychiatrist,
Midland Centre for Forensic Psychiatry,
All Saints' Hospital, Birmingham

Foreword by

Kenneth Rawnsley
CBE FRCP FRCPsych DPM
President of the Royal College of Psychiatrists
Professor of Psychological Medicine,
Welsh National School of Medicine

CHURCHILL LIVINGSTONE
EDINBURGH LONDON MELBOURNE AND NEW YORK 1983

CHURCHILL LIVINGSTONE
Medical Division of Longman Group UK Limited

Distributed in the United States of America by
Churchill Livingstone Inc., 650 Avenue of the Americas,
New York, 10011, and by associated companies,
branches and representatives throughout the world.

First published 1983
    Reprinted 1984 with additional information
    Reprinted 1986
    Reprinted 1988
    Reprinted 1992

ISBN 0-443-03017-0

British Library Cataloguing in Publication Data. A
catalogue record for this book is available from the
British Library.

Library of Congress Cataloging in Publication Data
Bluglass, Robert.
    A guide to the Mental Health Act 1983.

    Includes index.
    1. Mental health laws – Great Britain. 2. Insane –
Commitment and detention – Great Britain. I. Title.
[DNLM: 1. Great Britain – Mental Health Act. 1983.
2. Mental health services – Great Britain – Legislation.
WM 33 FA 1B6g]
KD3412.B55   1983   344.41'044   83-7635
                    344.10444

Produced by Longman Singapore Publishers Pte Ltd
Printed in Singapore

Foreword

If a civilised society is to be judged by the care bestowed upon its sick and disabled members, then the supreme test may be applied by scrutinising the arrangements for compulsory detention and treatment of the mentally disordered. By its nature, mental disorder may lead to clouding of awareness, an impairment of judgment or subjective distortion of reality which may place the patient at hazard. To deprive the individual in this case of his liberty for his own protection, or to compel treatment, involves a grave infringement of personal rights which must be subject to strict controls.

The Mental Health Act 1983 has refined and clarified existing provisions under its 1959 predecessor but in addition has broken new ground. Enhanced access to Mental Health Review Tribunals and the requirement for more frequent review of the need to renew compulsory powers of detention are examples of modification to existing arrangements. The sharp focus on consent to treatment; the mandatory second opinion for certain treatments and the establishment of a Mental Health Act Commission are novelties.

To the student of social affairs the year long passage of the new Bill through Parliament was a fascinating and at times exciting spectacle. In the debates battle was joined between those who wished to dispense with constraints wholesale and those whose pragmatic sense gave voice to the dangers of so doing. The current fashion of multidisciplinary team work in psychiatric practice was reflected in pressure for participation of nurses, psychologists, social workers and lay people in crucial decisions about detention and treatment. The monolithic authority of doctors was questioned repeatedly. Civil rights and anti-professional currents were running strongly. The compromise package which has emerged possesses features which are manifestly good, for example, the new Commission, but there are others which generate concern among many psychiatrists, such as the extension of mandatory second opinion requirements for certain treatments to patients 'not liable to be detained' and the new category of 'mental impairment'.

Professor Bluglass is eminently qualified to expound the complexities of the new legislation. As Chairman of the Royal College of Psychiatrists Working Party he spent many hours in committee, in the lobbies of Westminster and in the ring-side seats in the Chamber of Lords and Commons. He supported me in a crucial appearance before the Special Standing Committee of the Commons to give evidence. He speaks with authority about events leading up to the promulgation of the Bill in 1981 since he was personally involved in many of them. His translation of the convoluted legal forms of the Act into plain English, and his commentary, are born of an intense and intimate preoccupation with the substance of the legislation as it evolved. Even the experienced psychiatric traveller will need a guide through the thickets of this Act. Professor Bluglass has provided it.

Cardiff   K. Rawnsley
1983

Preface

Many different professions apply the powers given by the Mental Health Act or work under its authority. Many of them have a detailed knowledge of the commonly used Sections of the Act of 1959 derived from long experience and they have been familiar with its pages throughout their professional lives. The new Act bears a close resemblance to its predecessor, but it has been rearranged, rewritten, renumbered, contains much that is new and discards many provisions that have become redundant. Virtually every Section has changed in some respect.

This guide aims to assist all those who need to understand the new legislation and learn to find their way through it.

The book describes the historical background, some of the arguments, the influences and events that preceded the Act's publication. The chapters dealing with the Parts of the Act discuss the reasons for making alterations or introducing new provisions, the principal changes and improvements that have been made, and the present state of the law controlling the treatment of patients detained in hospital or under guardianship and the measures to protect their civil rights. The guide is intended to be comprehensive, although some technical details of very infrequent concern are omitted. This is an explanatory and simplified version of the legislation. For absolute accuracy the reader must turn to the Act of Parliament itself.

It is intended that this guide will be of value to psychiatrists and their trainees, to nurses, social workers, probation officers, administrators and to students in these fields. It will also be of assistance to 'approved doctors', prison medical officers and police surgeons, lawyers, members of Tribunals and all others who are concerned with the care of the mentally disordered.

The new Act is an event in the history of mental health care of the greatest importance. The creation of the Mental Health Act Commission, the new rules controlling consent to treatment, the improvements in the rights of patients will all have far-reaching effects on the standards of care and treatment in the decade ahead.

I have been privileged to have been closely involved in the lengthy discussions which preceded the new Act during the past 10 years, for much of this time as Chairman of committees of the Royal College of

Psychiatrists which produced many proposals for improvements and commented upon the options that were put forward by the DHSS and other bodies, for consideration. This was followed by an intense period of activity during the passage of the Amendment Bill through Parliament which gave me a unique opportunity to witness the complexities of the process and to take part in much of the related discussion and lobbying.

I gratefully acknowledge the co-operation and the part played by my colleagues during this period when we worked under the leadership of the President of the Royal College of Psychiatrists, Professor Kenneth Rawnsley who has kindly written a Foreword to this book. I would wish to mention in this context the co-operation of the officials of the DHSS, particularly Mr Norman Hale, Dr Pamela Mason and Mrs Pam Hurley and Mrs Elizabeth Hunter Johnston who dealt with a constant stream of enquiries and suggestions in such a friendly, helpful and tolerant way. I wish to acknowledge personally the co-operation and courtesy of Lord Hunter of Newington and Lord Richardson during the time that the Bill was before the House of Lords, and the Members of the House of Commons Standing Committee, particularly Mr Terry Davis MP, all of whom were always ready to listen to, and discuss our suggestions, even if they did not always agree with them.

I would also take the opportunity to record the underlying influence of Sir Ivor Batchelor, who first introduced me to the exciting interface between psychiatry and the law.

Finally, my thanks go to my wife, Kerry, for her tolerance and support during the time that I have been assisting at the birth of the Act and subsequently during the preparation of this book. To Mrs Marjorie Crowe who typed the drafts with such skill, accuracy and cheerful good humour I am especially grateful, as I am to Mrs Sylvia Hull of the publishers for her helpful support and encouragement.

I also wish to thank Miss Jacqueline Crowe for her assistance and Mrs Dilys Thomas for preparing the flow diagrams.

Birmingham 1983   Robert Bluglass

Contents

1 Background to the new Mental Health Act

THE EVOLUTION OF MENTAL HEALTH LEGISLATION

Early English legislation recognised some forms of mental disorder but it was mostly concerned with the control of the property of 'lunatics' or 'persons of unsound mind' (who were thought likely to recover or to have lucid intervals) and 'idiots' or 'natural fools' (who were presumed to be incurable). Only the grossly disordered were given recognition as they were potentially dangerous or annoying to others, and they were kept out of sight at home, or in 'private madhouses' run for profit by private individuals. Many others were also to be found in poor houses, workhouses or gaols. Some were admitted to Bethlem or to other voluntary institutions. *The Vagrancy Acts of 1713 and 1744* provided for the apprehension and detention of those who might be dangerous, on the order of two or more justices, and the *Madhouses Act of 1774* provided for minimum standards of care and for the control of private madhouses. Conditions for patients at that time were usually appalling and disturbing reports of improper detention aroused the increasing concern of the reformers of the period. From 1774 onwards three distinct aims characterised the reforming movement:

1. to prevent the physical ill-treatment of the mentally disordered;
2. to ensure that they were housed under suitable conditions and preferably in institutions properly provided for them;
3. to ensure that no sane person could be improperly detained on the grounds that he was mentally disordered.

The *County Asylums Act of 1808* removed the care of patients from private institutions by authorising the provision of special public 'asylums', initially to house four classes of patients in institutions established by the County authorities:

1. 'dangerous lunatics' detained under the Vagrancy Act of 1744
2. 'criminal lunatics' detained 'during His Majesty's pleasure' under the first *Criminal Lunatics Act of 1800*;
3. 'pauper lunatics' to be transferred from poorhouses;
4. 'non-pauper' or paying patients.

During the 83 years, 1808 to 1891 over twenty Acts of Parliament were passed dealing with the care of mentally disordered people in public or private institutions. There were also four consolidations of the law that had been passed at intervals during this period, the last being the *Lunacy Act 1890*. In the following 65 years up to 1955 there were a further seven Acts and numerous amendments, but no major overhaul or complete restatement of the law, and no consolidation into one statute of the laws that had been enacted since 1890.

The nineteenth century legislation gave authority for the detention of various categories of patient. In 1904 a *Royal Commission on the Care and Control of the Feebleminded (Report 1908)* was appointed to consider the needs of persons who were not so disordered as to be certifiable under the Lunacy Acts, and the need for special forms of treatment for them and for 'idiots'. Their report recommended new legislation and resulted in the first *Mental Deficiency Act (1913)* which applied to four classes of mental defectives, 'idiots, imbeciles, feebleminded persons and moral imbeciles'. The *Mental Deficiency Act 1927* replaced the term 'moral imbecile' by 'moral defective' and introduced new definitions which remained in force until 1959. These Acts authorised separate designated institutions for 'mentally defective patients' separating them for the first time from the mentally ill. (Eventually to become the hospitals for the mentally handicapped.)

The *Mental Treatment Act 1930*, which followed a *Royal Commission on Lunacy and Mental Disorder 1924–1926 (Report 1926)* amended the terminology of the Lunacy Act 1890 replacing 'lunatic', and 'asylum' by the terms 'person of unsound mind' and 'mental hospital', changes which the Medico–Psychological Association had been recommending since 1918. This Act provided for the first time for voluntary admission to mental hospitals, following experience of admitting patients to mental hospitals without certification which had been pioneered through administrative action in parts of Scotland during the last decade of the nineteenth century. Temporary status was established for those who could express neither willingness nor unwillingness to enter hospital and who were likely to require hospital treatment for no more than one year. The 1930 Act was a major advance in the development of mental health legislation. By 1957 75 per cent of all admissions to designated mental hospitals were voluntary and in some hospitals the rate was over 90 per cent. Patients previously excluded because they were not certifiable now received treatment in the early stages of illness. These improvements also paralleled the important advances in psychiatric treatment that were beginning to take place, including the use of electro-convulsive therapy, leucotomy, new drugs and the development of psycho-analysis.

However, although there were many more voluntary admissions the population of mental hospitals at any one time still consisted of about 70 per cent 'certified' patients and as many as 20 000 patients a year were being admitted compulsorily in 1956.

Until 1959 it was illegal to admit patients of 'unsound mind' to other than 'designated mental hospitals', but parts of these hospitals had in some instances been 'de-designated' (they were not then legally mental hospitals) and general hospitals were beginning to provide beds for 'neurosis patients' who could be admitted without any formality. In addition, some hospitals provided a 'long stay annexe' for elderly psychiatric patients requiring nursing care to avoid the formalities and stigma attached to the designated mental hospital.

The *National Health Service Act of 1946* made major changes to the administration of the mental health services. Most hospitals became the responsibility of the Minister of Health, but the psychiatric hospitals remained designated for the exclusive admission of the mentally ill or mentally 'defective' and voluntary patients continued to be required to sign forms declaring their desire to be received into a mental hospital for treatment.

THE ROYAL COMMISSION ON THE LAW RELATING TO MENTAL ILLNESS AND MENTAL DEFICIENCY 1954–1957

The Royal Commission was appointed at a time during the immediate post war era when attitudes to psychiatry and methods of treatment were rapidly changing. The status of psychiatry as a developing branch of medicine had been elevated by the progress made during the Second World War and there was a general optimism about the advances that were likely to be made in the near future. The amalgamation of psychiatric and other hospital services within the National Health Service encouraged the move to regard psychiatric disorder in the same way as physical illness and to remove the isolation and segregation of psychiatric patients and staff.

The Royal Commission was appointed in October 1953 by Sir Derek Walker-Smith, the Minister of Health. The Chairman was Lord Percy of Newcastle and the Commission was required to report on all aspects of the law and administrative machinery governing the certification, care, treatment and management of mentally ill and mentally defective persons in England and Wales.

The report of the *Royal Commission (The Percy Commission) (Report 1957)* and the published evidence presented to it was detailed and wide-ranging. All the previous legislation, built up over many years, was to be repealed and the keystone of the new legislation was to be the right of mentally ill patients to be cared for informally, in-so-far as this is possible. Compulsory procedures would be an adjunct to a voluntary system rather than the reverse which had characterised the previous legislation. Mental disorder was redefined in accordance with modern principles, hospitals were to be desegregated and the circumstances justifying compulsion were reviewed. New procedures for the compulsory detention of patients were recommended with the conclusion, in the face of conflicting evidence, that the procedure should be in the hands of individuals who have a knowledge and experience of the questions at issue. They considered that it was inappropriate for people who were not medically qualified to give an opinion on a patient's state of mind. The procedures to admit patients were, therefore, to be entrusted to doctors and social workers without the involvement of a magistrate. The legalistic approach was appropriate when society was to be protected from the 'lunatic', but now that the primary concern was for the individual patient, the need and justification for treatment was the most important factor. Safeguards against abuse or inappropriate detention were to be vested in an independent body, the Mental Health Review Tribunal, and the Board of Control was no longer needed to inspect hospitals on behalf of a Minister who was himself responsible for their management.

THE MENTAL HEALTH ACT 1959

Most of the recommendations of the Percy Commission were accepted by Parliament and included in the *1959 Mental Health Act*, which took effect from the 1st November 1960. It has been widely regarded as an enlightened and liberal statute which pioneered the informal admission system, improved the acceptability of psychiatric care and reduced, without entirely eliminating, the stigma attached to receiving it. Involuntary hospitalisation only on medical certification left control of the management of the patient's case in the hands of the medical profession, a move which was supported by the World Health Organization. It was a method thought to be favoured by many patients and it was adopted by the mental health legislation of about 50 per cent of the countries surveyed by the World Health Organization in 1955 (W.H.O. 1955) and 1975 (Curran and Harding 1978).

The proportion of informal patients in psychiatric hospitals rose steadily after 1930 from 30 per cent in 1955 to over 90 per cent in some hospitals by 1975. The trend was the same for the mentally handicapped as for the mentally ill. The influence and the opportunities for change provided by the 1959 Act were immense but were also paralleled and enhanced by the developments which continued in the fields of psycho-pharmacology, ideas about community care, the advent of the open-door hospital and the movement towards multidisciplinary team management.

However, the Act was not without its critics. Informal patients remained covered by many of the restrictions applying to other patients in mental hospitals; the operation of the procedures was sometimes seen as loosely controlled. Some procedures, such as emergency admission were thought to be used for convenience rather than necessity, and offender-patients were increasingly refused admission on the grounds that facilities for their care did not exist. There were periodic accusations of bad care or practice in psychiatric hospitals which resulted in some fourteen major and expensive enquiries (and numerous minor ones) which some writers considered was the price paid for disbanding the Board of Control. Much of this was seen as a reflection of unsatisfactory management and a serious lack of resources, rather than resulting from any serious defect of principle in the Act itself, but there was a growing recognition that forms of inspectorate are indispensable to raise, or maintain standards of care and to draw Government attention to major deficiencies. The Health Advisory Service (previously the Hospital Advisory Service) was established to visit and report on conditions in hospitals, to disseminate 'good practice' on behalf of the Secretary of State. The National Development Team visits mental handicap hospitals to advise on management and practice. These bodies are concerned with management and the delivery of services; individual patients now also have access to the independent Parliamentary Health Service Commissioner to voice complaints. Private nursing homes are subject to independent statutory inspection by the Department of Health and Social Security. In addition, patients may ultimately take a complaint to the European Court of Human Rights which the United Kingdom has endorsed and in recent years, have increasingly done so. It is noteworthy that Scotland was provided with a Mental Welfare Commission by the *Mental Health (Scotland) Act 1960* and it is remarkable that a body thought necessary for the Scots, which continued to have an independent responsibility for individual patients as well as service provision, was not provided for the English and Welsh.

THE ORIGINS OF THE NEW LEGISLATION

Despite the undoubted benefits of the 1959 Act, the growth of the civil rights movement in the 1960's led to a new period of criticism and disenchantment with what was regarded as medical paternalism and an excessive reliance on psychiatric judgment. This movement, so far as the mentally disordered were concerned, began in the United States of America where the courts were used as a forum for the mentally ill and mentally handicapped. There were a series of legal decisions which endorsed the right to active treatment of mentally disordered patients (rather than simply to be held in custody). Other decisions specifically concerned mentally handicapped patients and confirmed their right to adequate standards of care, to education, protection from exploitation and the right to privacy. Further decisions for the mentally ill included the right to communicate, to correspond freely, to personal property, to vote, to employment (where possible), to education, to independent psychiatric examination, to consent to treatment and many others. These decisions indicated that mental disorder, and even compulsory detention, does not necessarily imply incompetency in every aspect of life and that new legislation was required to protect the individual patient and to preserve his independence and civil liberties.

In England, the professionals were themselves well aware of the need to review the operation of the 1959 Act and in 1972 the Royal College of Psychiatrists formed a committee to consider in what areas improvements and changes could be recommended. The National Association for Mental Health (MIND) representing the consumer, also carried out a review under the leadership of an American lawyer, Mr Larry Gostin, its Legal Director. Gostin published two reports (Gostin 1975; Gostin 1977) which suggested that the 1959 Act was over-restrictive, gave the patients too few opportunities to appeal against detention and was too heavily controlled by the medical profession. There is no doubt that Gostin's writings and campaigning zeal were a crucial influence leading to an eventual change in the law. The British Association of Social Workers (BASW), the British Psychological Society and the Royal Society for Mentally Handicapped Adults and Children (MENCAP) also joined those exerting pressure for change.

REPORTS AND RESPONSES 1975–1981

The *Committee on Mentally Abnormal Offenders* chaired by Lord Butler of Saffron Walden had reported in 1975 (Home Office and DHSS 1975) on the law and services relating to abnormal offenders and had included a review of Part V of the 1959 Act, which is concerned with offender-patients, making important recommendations for a change in the law.

In response to the pressure groups, the Government of the day set up an interdepartmental committee in 1974 representing the Department of Health and Social Security, the Home Office, the Lord Chancellor's Department and the Welsh Office to consider all the suggestions that had been made to amend the Act and to present conflicting arguments and alternative proposals for debate. A Consultative Document was issued in 1976 (DHSS 1976). There were published responses from the main organisations and a multidisciplinary conference was held, chaired by the Secretary of State, Mr David Ennals. The Government subsequently published a White Paper in September 1978 (DHSS, Home Office, Welsh Office and Lord Chancellor's Department 1978) with its proposals for an Amendment Bill. Many of the proposals were generally accepted, but MIND and BASW were disappointed and considered the suggestions too timid. The Royal College of Psychiatrists and the medical profession, although accepting many of the proposals, strongly resisted the recommendation for a lay panel to monitor the patient's consent to psychiatric treatment and regretted that a proposal to return to an independent commission like the old Board of Control had been rejected as incompatible with the principle that psychiatric patients should be dealt with, as far as it is possible, in the same way as those who are physically ill.

The return of a new Government in 1979 allowed a reconsideration of the more controversial 1978 proposals and following a period of intensive informal discussions, a *Mental Health (Amendment) Bill* was published on 11th November 1981, together with an explanatory White Paper, *'Reform of Mental Health Legislation'*. (DHSS, Home Office, Welsh Office and Lord Chancellor's Department 1981.)

THE MENTAL HEALTH (AMENDMENT) BILL

The main objects of the 1981 Bill were to improve the safeguards for detained patients, to clarify the position of staff looking after them and to remove uncertainties in the law as represented by the 1959 Mental Health Act. The Amendment Bill was not a new statement or philosophy of the law, but a set of proposals to update and improve the existing Act which had stood the test of time.

Many of the proposals were carried over from the previous Government's 1978 White Paper and were non-controversial. There were new proposals which met with general approval, the most important of which was the establishment of a new Mental Health Act Commission, originally proposed by the Royal College of Psychiatrists, to be concerned primarily with the interests and protection of individual detained patients. Proposals to control the position on consent to treatment were the most controversial clauses in the 1981 Bill and were regarded as too restrictive and impracticable by the medical profession and insufficiently independent of medical control by the lay pressure groups. At a later stage, following intensive lobbying and an evaluation of the way in which new initial rules might operate (Beedie & Bluglass 1982), the Government put forward a new series of more moderate and sensible proposals which were eventually accepted by Parliament.

The Bill had its first reading in the House of Lords (11th November 1981) and finished its passage there on 4th March 1982, after nearly 29 hours of debate during its various stages. The Government's proposals were skilfully advanced by Lord Elton and a high standard of discussion and concern for the psychiatric patients was expressed by peers who attended in considerable numbers throughout the passage of the Bill. 198 amendments to the Bill were proposed at various stages and 119, more than half, were agreed.

The Bill moved to the House of Commons in April 1982. A special procedure was operated for the detailed examination of the Bill at the Committee stage of its passage. A Special Standing Committee of 17 Members of Parliament and a Chairman was appointed for this purpose, which first invited evidence from concerned individuals and organisations, and witnesses were requested to attend before the Committee and were examined. This procedure greatly improved the knowledge and insight of the M.P.'s who exhibited an outstanding level of understanding and mastery of the issues concerned during their subsequent sittings. The Committee sat on 22 occasions between 22nd April 1982 and 29th June 1982 and was mainly responsible for the final shape of the Bill. It was observed on several occasions by Members of Parliament that it is very unusual for legislation to be so thoroughly and impartially examined as was the case here and scrutiny of the reported debates will confirm that contributions and concessions were made by both Government and opposition parties working for the most part in accord, sometimes to the dismay of one or other of the professional groups following the proceedings.

By the time the Bill had completed its passage through the Commons a further 100 or more amendments were passed, so that the appearance of the Bill had changed considerably by the time it returned to the House of Lords for its final scrutiny. The Bill received the Royal Assent on 28th October 1982 and became the Mental Health (Amendment) Act, to operate from 30th September 1983.

The Mental Health Bill published early in 1983, now the Mental Health Act 1983, is a consolidation measure, which brings together in one statute the 1959 Act as amended by the Mental Health (Amendment) Act.

REFERENCES

Beedie M A, Bluglass R 1982 Consent to psychiatric treatment: practical implications of the Mental Health (Amendment) Bill. British Medical Journal 284: 1613–1616

Curran A J, Harding T W 1978 The law and mental health: harmonizing objectives. World Health Organization, Geneva

DHSS, Home Office 1975 Report of the Committee on Mentally Abnormal Offenders (Chairman, Lord Butler of Saffron Walden) Cmnd 6244 HMSO London

DHSS 1976 A Review of the Mental Health Act 1959 (The Consultative Document) HMSO London

DHSS, Home Office, Welsh Office, Lord Chancellor's Department 1978 Review of the Mental Health Act 1959 Cmnd 7320 HMSO London (White Paper 1978)

DHSS, Home Office, Welsh Office, Lord Chancellor's Department 1981 Reform of Mental Health Legislation Cmnd 8405 HMSO London (White Paper 1981)

Gostin L O 1975 A human condition 1. National Association of Mental Health London

Gostin L O 1977 A human condition 2. National Association of Mental Health London

McGarry A L, Kaplan H A 1973 Overview: current trends in mental health law. American Journal of Psychiatry 130 6 621

Royal Commission on the Care and Control of the Feebleminded 1904–1908 1908 (Chairman, Lord Radnor) Cmnd 4202 HMSO London

Royal Commission on Lunacy and Mental Disorder 1924–1926 1926 (Chairman H P Macmillan) Report Cmnd 2700 HMSO London

Royal Commission on the law relating to Mental Illness and Mental Deficiency 1954–1957 1957 (Chairman Lord Percy of Newcastle) Report Cmnd 169 HMSO London

World Health Organization 1955 Hospitalisation of mental patients. A survey of existing legislation. International Digest of Health Legislation 6: 3–100 Geneva

World Health Organization Expert Committee on Mental Health 1955 Legislation affecting psychiatric treatment World Health Organization Technical Report Series 98 Geneva

FURTHER READING

Hoenig J, Hamilton M H 1969 The desegregation of the mentally ill. Routledge and Kegan Paul London

Hunter R A, McAlpine I 1963 Three hundred years of psychiatry. Oxford University Press Oxford

Jones K 1972 A history of the mental health services. Routledge and Kegan Paul London

2 Introduction to the Act

The Mental Health Act 1983 represents the Mental Health Act of 1959 as amended by the Mental Health (Amendment) Act. The 1983 Act also incorporates amendments that were made over the years to its predecessor by 28 other Acts of Parliament which make reference to the Mental Health Act, but it is principally derived from the 1959 and 1982 Acts of Parliament.

In drafting this *consolidation* Act, Parliament has taken the opportunity to clarify the legislation and rearrange the order of Parts and Sections, presumably with the anticipation that it will be easier for the practitioner to follow. As a consequence the numbering of Sections, previously so familiar to those who regularly used the Act, has changed. The chapters of this guide are presented in a broadly similar sequence for ease of reference but occasionally discussion of a later Section is included with an earlier one in an attempt to achieve greater clarification.

PARTS OF THE ACT

The Parts of the Mental Health Act 1983 are arranged as follows:

PART I	APPLICATION OF ACT
PART II	COMPULSORY ADMISSION TO HOSPITAL AND GUARDIANSHIP
PART III	PATIENTS CONCERNED IN CRIMINAL PROCEEDINGS OR UNDER SENTENCE
PART IV	CONSENT TO TREATMENT
PART V	MENTAL HEALTH REVIEW TRIBUNALS
PART VI	REMOVAL AND RETURN OF PATIENTS WITHIN THE UNITED KINGDOM ETC
PART VII	MANAGEMENT OF PROPERTY AND AFFAIRS OF PATIENTS
PART VIII	MISCELLANEOUS FUNCTIONS OF LOCAL AUTHORITIES AND THE SECRETARY OF STATE
PART IX	OFFENCES
PART X	MISCELLANEOUS AND SUPPLEMENTARY

The Act includes 149 Sections. The Sections corresponding with those in the 1959 Act with which users were most familiar are shown in the following table:

Table 2.1 Principal corresponding sections in the 1983 and 1959 Mental Health Acts

MENTAL HEALTH ACT 1983 SECTION	MENTAL HEALTH ACT 1959 SECTION
1 Definition of mental disorder	4
2 Admission for assessment	25
3 Admission for treatment	26
4 Emergency admission	29
5 Detention of informal patient	30
6 Effect of application for admission	31
7 Application for guardianship	33
8 Effect of application for guardianship	34
12 Approval of doctors	28
37 Hospital & guardianship orders	60
41 Restriction orders	65
47 Transfer of prisoners to hospital	72
48 Other prisoners to hospital	73
49 Restrictions on prisoners	74
135 Searching for and removing patients	135
136 Mentally disturbed patients in public places	136
139 Protection for staff	141

The basic philosophy of the new mental health legislation remains as it has been for the past 24 years. In so far as it is possible, psychiatric care is to be obtained in the community and informally. Section 131 emphasises that 'nothing in the Act shall be construed as preventing a patient who requires treatment from being admitted to any hospital or mental nursing home ... without any application, order or direction rendering him liable to be detained under this Act, or from remaining in any hospital or nursing home ... after he has ceased to be liable to be detained'. This Section also states (131(b)) that in the case of a person of 16 years or over, capable of expressing his own wishes, any such informal arrangements may be made, carried out and determined, 'not withstanding any right of custody or control' vested by law in his parent or guardian. Much of the Act is, therefore, concerned with the relatively small proportion of psychiatric patients who require to be detained in hospital or to be placed under guardianship in their own interests.

The subsequent chapters discuss the background to the main Parts of the Act, describe the principal changes which have been introduced to improve and update the 1959 Act and then attempt to clarify the provisions of each Section bringing together at one point, associated matters such as, for instance, the right to a Tribunal application, or the duties of doctor or social worker.

Some useful addresses and telephone numbers are included in the Appendix, with a glossary of definitions.

Transitional arrangements

The Act provides for a phasing-in period which retains the current status and certain rights of patients who were in hospital under the provisions of the 1959 Act at the time that the 1983 Act came into operation. No attempt has been made to discuss these arrangements in this Guide and the reader is referred to Schedule 5 of the Mental Health Act 1983.

Note

It should be reiterated that the following discussion is not in every respect a precise reproduction of the wording of each Section of the Act, although every effort has been made to avoid errors of fact and meaning. Where absolute accuracy is required the reader must consult the statute.

REFERENCE
DHSS 1983 Mental Health Act 1983: Explanatory memorandum. DHSS London.

3 The definition of mental disorder (Part I) Section 1

BACKGROUND

This was *previously Section 4, MHA 1959*.

The *Mental Health Act 1959* defined mental disorder as:

> 'Mental illness, arrested or incomplete development of mind, psychopathic disorder and any other disorder or disability of mind'.

Two of these forms of mental disorder were defined further:

1. 'arrested or incomplete development of mind' which had two sub-categories: subnormality and severe subnormality;
2. psychopathic disorder.

MENTAL ILLNESS

Mental illness was not further defined in the *1959 Act* as it is a term which covers a wide range of dissimilar illnesses, which may require treatment in hospital, and it is a term which is in general medical use. The Mental Health Act 1983 has not changed this approach and mental illness remains undefined.

THE EXCLUSION OF MENTAL HANDICAP (SUBNORMALITY)

The previous Government proposed replacing the terms 'subnormality' and 'severe subnormality' with 'mental handicap' and 'severe mental handicap', terms which have gained general usage (as in 'hospital for the mentally handicapped') and which seem to describe more appropriately the condition of one particular group of patients. The terms subnormality and severe subnormality were considered to be pejorative, out-of-date and to tend to cause offence and distress. Mental handicap and severe mental handicap were to be further defined to reflect the contemporary view that this is a condition that may be described equally in terms of limitation of intelligence, social functioning and behaviour. These proposals appeared to be generally welcomed.

Initially, similar recommendations were made for the present legislation after the Government had decided that it was still appropriate to provide some compulsory powers for mentally handicapped people. A very small proportion of patients in hospitals for the mentally handicapped are detained, usually for their own safety, and compulsory powers for this group would continue to be needed and would also be required to place such patients under guardianship. Immediately prior to the introduction of the Mental Health Act 1983, under three per cent of the admissions to mental handicap hospitals and units in England and Wales were compulsory.

However, after the introduction of the Amendment Bill in the House of Lords, arguments were presented on behalf of a number of organisations, but notably the Royal Society for Mentally Handicapped Children and Adults (MENCAP), a voluntary body, to remove the term 'mental handicap' entirely from the new legislation. It was considered that the inclusion of mental handicap with mental illness in the same statute leads to confusion in the public mind and suggests that the two conditions are synonymous, or that the mentally handicapped may be detained compulsorily simply because of the presence of mental handicap in isolation, uncomplicated by any concurrent mental illness. This is, of course, a misunderstanding; the presence of any form of mental disorder does not by itself warrant compulsory hospital admission, other criteria must also be met.

MENCAP stressed its view that mental handicap is not an illness but a disability akin to physical handicap and that it is a condition that can usually benefit from care or training either on a voluntary basis or in the community. Some claimed that compulsory admission is never justified, although the Royal College of Psychiatrists disagreed and stated that there is a very small minority of mentally handicapped people without any mental illness who need to be detained in hospital. Despite this, the case presented by MENCAP was argued with force in the House of Lords and the Government, which had earlier offered to separate mental handicap from the rest of the Act by confining mention of it to a separate Part, later agreed to give the proposal to exclude it altogether further consideration. If this was to be accepted, however, an alternative method of detaining some patients had to be devised.

PRINCIPAL CHANGES

THE NEW CONCEPT OF MENTAL IMPAIRMENT

1. It was subsequently decided that a new term 'mental impairment'* could be used to distinguish that small group of mentally handicapped people who need to be detained in hospital or received into guardianship from the majority who do not. The words used to define 'mental impairment' and 'severe mental impairment' were selected with care, including restrictions to limit the effect of the Act

* 'Impairment' means here 'any loss or abnormality of psychological, physiological or anatomical structure or function'. It is derived from the *International Classification of Impairments, Disabilities and Handicaps.* World Health Organization, Geneva 1980.

on handicapped people to those for whom treatment in hospital is the only alternative, and a more appropriate form of care than prison.

2. To justify inclusion in the category of mental impairment the individual must not only suffer from *severe* or *significant* impairment of intelligence and social functioning, but such a degree of handicap must also be associated with abnormally aggressive or seriously irresponsible conduct on the part 'of the person concerned'. (Not yet 'patient' as the individual is assumed by the legislators not yet to be under medical care.) Reference to the treatability of the condition, previously part of the definition, is now removed and is more logically included among the criteria necessary for the compulsory admission of a patient.

The new legislation has, therefore, created a new category of patient in order that the majority of mentally handicapped patients might be protected from prejudicial identification with patients suffering from mental illness. Although this strategy received general support in both Houses of Parliament, the Royal College of Psychiatrists and MIND both expressed doubts about the wisdom of this move, not only on semantic grounds, but also fearing that the well-intentioned efforts to improve the status of mentally handicapped patients in the community might lead to an attitude of prejudice, rejection and alienation of the new group of mentally impaired patients in hospital, particularly when these patients are at the stage of returning to the community (when they will, in due course, be termed 'mentally handicapped' again).

The definitions will be seen to be more closely associated with the definition of psychopathic disorder, despite the different aetiology and behaviour patterns of the two conditions, although it may be noted that the Percy Commission made little or no distinction between 'feebleminded persons or moral defectives' and inadequate and aggressive psychopaths, but the subsequent Mental Health Act 1959 divided these groups into 'subnormality' and 'psychopathic disorder'.

3. The term 'arrested or incomplete development of mind' in the generic definition of mental disorder remains, so that for short-term compulsory admission (Sections 2, 4, 5, 135, 136) requiring only a diagnosis of 'mental disorder', individuals suffering only from 'arrested or incomplete development of mind', that is to say uncomplicated mental handicap, are, by definition included. For the longer-term sections (Section 3, 7, 37, 38) a diagnosis of mental impairment or severe mental impairment must be made if it is appropriate to support an application for admission to hospital or guardianship.

4. Mental handicap and severe mental handicap still appeared in the Mental Health (Amendment) Act, in Schedule 3. This part of the Act described the amendments to other Acts of Parliament which were necessary as a result of the changes made to mental health legislation (consequential amendments). These are Acts which rely

on a cross-reference to the Mental Health (Amendment) Act and include the Sexual Offences Act 1967 and the Juries Act 1974. In relation to these statutes mental handicap and severe mental handicap remain appropriate terms, as they do for general usage in England and Wales.

PSYCHOPATHIC DISORDER

Background

The *1959 Act* defined psychopathic disorder as:

> 'a persistent disorder or disability of mind (whether or not including subnormality of intelligence) which results in abnormally aggressive or seriously irresponsible conduct on the part of the patient and requires or is susceptible to medical treatment'.

This definition had a complex historical background which has been cogently described in the Butler Report of the Committee of Mentally Abnormal Offenders and which is generally considered to be largely attributable to the late Professor Sir Denis Hill, the distinguished psychiatrist, who was one of the Committee members. The Committee remarked on the continuing diversity of opinion as to the nature of this condition, the lack of material progress in provision for the diagnosis and treatment of psychopathic conditions, and continuing uncertainty and doubt about the treatability of the various states that are encompassed by the term 'psychopathic disorder'. The Committee considered that any ambiguity about the responsibility of prisons to cater for offenders with dangerous anti-social tendencies, which might exist as a result of the power to send those suffering from psychopathic disorder to hospital under Section 60 (1) of the Mental Health Act 1959 should be removed. Special units should be set up in prisons for the training and treatment of psychopaths. There are, however, some psychopathic patients who may respond to treatment and some hospitals and doctors prepared to accept them. It was, therefore, concluded that psychopathic disorder should remain within the scope of the Act, even though many witnesses had urged the Butler Committee to suggest that this disorder should be removed from the definitions of mental disorder in mental health legislation, and the arguments for this were summarised in detail.

The Butler Committee also wished to see psychopathic disorder replaced by the less damaging term 'personality disorder'; but this had little subsequent support although it was given some consideration during the debates preceding the new legislation.

Principal change

When the new legislation was under review the doubts expressed by the Butler Committee were generally supported and it was decided to retain psychopathic disorder in the Act, but the view of the previous Government (White Paper 1978), that the compulsory detention of psychopaths should be dependent upon a good prospect of benefit from treatment, was also accepted. The *diagnosis* has now been separated from *susceptibility to treatment* in the definition.

There was very little discussion of this matter in either House of Parliament and the revised definition of psychopathic disorder was accepted.

SEXUAL DEVIANCY AND DRUG OR ALCOHOL DEPENDENCE

Background
The *1959 Act* indicated that no-one may be dealt with under the powers of the Act 'by reason only of promiscuity or other immoral conduct'.

The Butler Committee recommended that similarly it would be wrong to allow the use of compulsory powers for the admission of sexual deviants, alcoholics or drug addicts. Sexual deviancy is not now considered to be a mental disorder in itself. Alcoholics and drug addicts have sometimes in the past been admitted for short periods for observation on the basis that they were suffering from 'any other disorder or disability of mind'. This is now thought to be inappropriate as these conditions are regarded as social and behaviour problems rather than mental disorders. If they subsequently lead to the development of a mental disorder then compulsory admission might, in some cases, be justified.

Principal change
The new Act includes the principle that no one should be admitted to hospital compulsorily because of the existence of sexual deviance, alcohol dependence or drug addiction alone. It is possible to detain a person on the grounds of co-existing mental disorder or where one of these conditions is a symptom of demonstrable mental disorder within the meaning of the Act.

DEFINITION OF MENTAL DISORDER: MENTAL HEALTH ACT 1983 SECTION 1

The revised definition of mental disorder in the Mental Health Act 1983 is as follows:

1. In this Act *'mental disorder'* means mental illness, arrested or incomplete development of mind, psychopathic disorder and any other disorder or disability of mind; and *'mentally disordered'* shall be construed accordingly.
2. In this Act *'severe mental impairment'* means a state of arrested or incomplete development of mind which includes severe impairment of intelligence and social functioning and is associated with abnormally aggressive or seriously irresponsible conduct on the part of the person concerned.
3. In this Act *'mental impairment'* means a state of arrested or incomplete development of mind (not amounting to severe mental

impairment) which includes significant impairment of intelligence and social functioning and is associated with abnormally aggressive or seriously irresponsible conduct on the part of the person concerned.

4. In this Act *'psychopathic disorder'* means a persistent disorder or disability of mind (whether or not including significant impairment of intelligence) which results in abnormally aggressive or seriously irresponsible conduct on the part of the person concerned.

5. Nothing in this section shall be construed as implying that a person may be dealt with under this Act as suffering from mental disorder or from any form of mental disorder described in this section, by reason only of promiscuity or other immoral conduct, sexual deviancy or dependence on alcohol or drugs.

4 Compulsory admission to hospital (Part II)

BACKGROUND

The power to detain a patient in hospital compulsorily is an authority that must be used with restraint and caution. An important distinguishing feature of the English legislation is that compulsory committal does not involve any judicial authority, whereas in many countries, including Scotland, a judge must approve the recommendation that a person's mental state justifies curtailing his freedom by detaining him in hospital. In England and Wales, since 1959, the responsibility has been given to the doctors, social workers and hospital managers. The relatives have certain rights to discharge the patient and there are opportunities which are now increased to appeal to a Mental Health Review Tribunal against committal.

The patient should always be admitted informally, if this is possible. Compulsory action is clearly a serious step involving deprivation of liberty, restriction of individual rights and freedom of action. The procedures now to be followed are designed to ensure that the mental state and forms of behaviour which justify compulsion are clearly defined and that alternative forms of management and treatment are carefully considered. Although the grounds for compulsory admission are clarified they are also rather more restrictive than before with an emphasis upon treatability.

It should be noted that immediately prior to the commencement of the 1983 legislation 10 per cent of admissions to mental illness hospitals and units in England and Wales were compulsory.

ADMISSION FOR ASSESSMENT (SECTION 2)

(previously Section 25 MHA 1959)

PRINCIPAL CHANGES

1. Previously this Section allowed compulsory admission for observation (with or without medical treatment). In recent years some nurses and doctors have been increasingly uncertain about the authority given by the Act to treat a patient while he is detained 'for observation'. The Section is re-worded to make it clear that the

purpose of admission is the *assessment* of the patient, and that *treatment can be given* during a 28-day period.

2. When the application is made by an Approved Social Worker, the Officer will now be required to take such steps as are practicable to inform the nearest relative that the patient has been, or will be, admitted to hospital.

3. The nearest relative, in addition to the Responsible Medical Officer and the hospital managers, has a new right to discharge the patient.

4. Treatment is subject to the 'consent to treatment' restrictions.

5. The patient, but not the nearest relative, has a new right of appeal to the Mental Health Review Tribunal within 14 days of admission. (Any longer period would have been impracticable.)

Purpose
To admit a patient to hospital for assessment (or for assessment followed by medical treatment) for 28 days.

Grounds
a. He is suffering from a mental disorder of a nature or degree which warrants the detention of the patient in a hospital for assessment (or for assessment followed by medical treatment) for at least a limited period; and
b. that he ought to be so detained in the interests of his own health or safety or with a view to the protection of other persons.

Medical recommendations
Two medical practitioners (one an 'approved' doctor), who both agree and state that the two grounds for making the recommendation are complied with. They should have examined the patient either together or separately, but in the latter case not more than five clear days should have elapsed between the two examinations (see page 27).

Applications
May be made by the nearest relative (see Chapter 10 for definitions) or Approved Social Worker either of whom must have seen the patient within 14 days ending with the date of the application. So far as it is practicable and would not involve undue delay, the Officer should consult the nearest relative before making an application. Where this has not been possible, the Officer must, before or within a reasonable time, take such steps as are practicable to inform the nearest relative that the application is, or has been made and of the nearest relative's power to discharge the patient.

A nearest relative who desires that an application for admission to hospital for assessment be made is entitled to apply to the hospital managers, or to the Local Authority Social Services Department, for a direction that an Approved Social Worker will investigate the proposed application as soon as it is practicable. If subsequently an application is not made the reason must be recorded and sent to the nearest relative.

Duration

Twenty-eight days, beginning with the day of admission. The patient must be discharged at the end of this period unless further powers of detention have been taken.

Powers of discharge

The doctor in charge of the case, the hospital managers or the nearest relative may discharge the patient, but the managers may prevent the discharge by the nearest relative if the doctor in charge of the case certifies that the patient is dangerous. In this case the nearest relative may apply to a Tribunal within 28 days. The patient may apply to a Mental Health Review Tribunal within the first 14 days of detention.

ADMISSION FOR TREATMENT (SECTION 3)

(previously Section 26)

PRINCIPAL CHANGES

1. The grounds upon which a patient can be compulsorily detained for treatment have been altered. As previously, the specific forms of mental disorder must be specified and it is not possible to admit a patient on the grounds that he is suffering only from 'any other disorder or disability of mind'. The mental disorder must be of a nature or degree which makes hospital admission the only appropriate method of management.

2. The age limits for the admission of psychopathic and subnormal patients are removed and replaced by a 'treatability' requirement; that in the case of psychopathic disorder or mental impairment the treatment is likely to alleviate or prevent a deterioration of the condition. Such patients should only be admitted if there is a prospect of benefit from the proposed treatment, either by giving the patient relief, or assisting him to adjust more satisfactorily in the community, or by preventing a worsening of his condition.

3. It is more clearly specified that admission for treatment must also be necessary for the health or safety of the patient, or the protection of other persons, and that treatment could only be provided by compulsory hospital admission if informal admission is impracticable.

4. The period of initial and subsequent detention under this Section is now six months (previously one year), a further six months (previously a further year) and then for one year at a time (previously every two years).

5. The 'consent to treatment' arrangements apply to patients detained under Section 3 (see page 79).

6. Patients may appeal to the Mental Health Review Tribunal within each six-month period, but the hospital managers must refer to the Tribunal the case of any patient who has been detained for the first period of six months and has not exercised his right of appeal.

Purpose
The compulsory admission of a patient for the treatment of his mental disorder.

Grounds
a. He is suffering from mental illness, severe mental impairment, psychopathic disorder or mental impairment of a nature or degree which makes it appropriate for him to receive medical treatment in hospital; and
b. in the case of psychopathic disorder or mental impairment that such treatment is likely to alleviate or prevent a deterioration of his condition; and
c. that it is necessary for the health or safety of other persons that he should receive such treatment, and that it cannot be provided unless he is detained under this Section.

Medical recommendations
Two doctors (one 'approved') who have personally examined the patient either together or separately. Where they have examined the patient separately, not more than five days must have elapsed between the two examinations.

Applications
The nearest relative of the patient or an Approved Social Worker who must consult the nearest relative if it is possible to do so. An objection from the nearest relative prevents the Approved Social Worker making the application. The applicant must have personally seen the patient within the previous 14 days.

Duration
Six months unless renewed for a further six months by the Responsible Medical Officer (see page 37) and then at annual intervals.

Powers of discharge
The patient may be discharged by the Responsible Medical Officer, by the managers of the hospital or by the nearest relative of the patient, having given 72 hours notice (unless the RMO has certified that the patient is dangerous).

In the latter case the nearest relative may apply to a Mental Health Review Tribunal, on the patient's behalf, within 28 days of being so informed.

The patient may appeal to a Mental Health Review Tribunal within six months of admission. If he does not do so and is detained for a further six months, the managers of the hospital must automatically refer his case to the Tribunal.

ADMISSION IN AN EMERGENCY (SECTION 4)

(previously Section 29, MHA 1959)

PRINCIPAL CHANGES

1. The applicants are now restricted to the nearest relative (rather

than any relative) or an Approved Social Worker. Any relative was considered to wide a provision.

2. The person making the application must have seen the patient personally within the previous 24 hours. This is to ensure that the Section is only used in genuine emergencies and where it is not possible, or there is not time, to seek a second medical opinion.

3. The application must be acted on and the patient conveyed to hospital within 24 hours beginning at the time when the patient was medically examined or beginning at the time the application was made (whichever is the earlier).

4. This Section does not come within the consent to treatment requirements which only apply to the Sections of the Act which allow the detention of patients for treatment. However, any treatment of urgent necessity may be given with the authority of common law, which would be applicable to relieve serious suffering, or to save the patient's life or prevent a deterioration in an urgent situation. The decision is a matter for the doctor who must take account of all the circumstances.

5. There are no powers of appeal.

Purpose
Emergency application for admission for assessment.

Grounds
It is of urgent necessity for the patient to be admitted and detained in hospital under Section 4 of the Act (and for the reasons given under Section 2).

Medical recommendations
May be limited to one of the doctors required to give the two recommendations under Section 2, and if possible, by a doctor who previously knew the patient (usually the family doctor), and the patient must be admitted within 24 hours of the examination (or of the application if made earlier).

Applications
The nearest relative or an Approved Social Worker either of whom must have seen the patient within the previous 24 hours.

Duration
Seventy-two hours from the time of admission.

Powers of discharge
The patient must be discharged after 72 hours unless a second medical recommendation is received and that, with the first recommendation, the requirements for detention under Section 2 are complied with.

PATIENTS ALREADY IN HOSPITAL (SECTION 5)

(previously Section 30, MHA 1959)

PRINCIPAL CHANGES

1. This Section of the Act provides for the detention of an informal patient already under care in a hospital or unit (whether or not a psychiatric unit) who has indicated his intention of leaving hospital. He may be detained if it is considered that he would be a danger to himself or others if allowed to leave. In these circumstances the doctor in charge of the patient's treatment can report to the managers that an application for admission to hospital ought to be made and this Section authorises the detention of the patient in hospital for 72 hours (previously three days) from the time that the report is made.

    This period of detention gives time for the full application procedure (involving the nearest relative or Approved Social Worker and another doctor) to be completed.

2. There have been irregularities in the operation of this power of detention in the past, particularly when there have been difficulties in the doctor in charge of the case attending immediately. Yet there has been no legal power under the 1959 Act for another doctor to act in the absence of the doctor in charge of the case.

    Under the new legislation the doctor in charge of the patient may nominate a suitably qualified deputy (to be defined) on the staff of the hospital, to act in his absence for the purpose of detaining a patient under Section 5. The deputising doctor is required to exercise his own clinical judgement, not simply to carry out the instructions of the doctor in charge of the patient at a distance. Only one deputy may be nominated.

3. Some organisations representing nurses, particularly the Confederation of Health Service Employees (COHSE), had expressed concern and uncertainty about the authority and powers of nurses to detain patients while a doctor is found. There is a common law protection for staff, who, consistent with training and experience, and acting in good faith, detain informal patients who are considered to be at risk themselves or who are a danger to others*. However, COHSE did not feel that this was sufficient protection in some circumstances and that the Act should make the legal position of nurses quite clear. The 1983 Act, therefore, authorises psychiatric nurses of a prescribed class (to be defined clearly by Secretary of State's Order) to hold the patient for up to six hours if certain conditions (see below) are satisfied. This holding power ceases on the arrival of the doctor and the 72 hour detention under Section 5 includes any period of detention under the 'holding power'. These

---

*HC(76)11 The Management of Violent and Potentially Violent patients in hospital (DHSS Circular) 1976

arrangements are intended to give support to nurses and to enable them to obtain medical support within a reasonable time.

It should be noted, however, that although this Section can be used in any ward of any hospital, only *psychiatric* nurses may operate the holding power provided by the Act and only in respect of patients receiving treatment for Mental Disorder. In a general medical or surgical ward doctors are likely to attend quickly and nurses acting in good faith will be protected by the common law.

Purpose
The detention, where necessary, of a patient already receiving treatment in hospital as an in-patient.

Grounds
If it appears that an application for the admission of a patient to a hospital should be made. (That the patient may be a danger to himself or others).

Medical recommendations
The doctor in charge of the case or his nominated deputy.

Application
By report in writing from the doctor in charge of the patient's treatment to the managers of the hospital.

Duration
Seventy-two hours from the time that the report is made (or from the commencement of a nurse's 'holding power').

Discharge
The patient must be discharged at the end of 72 hours unless further powers of detention have been taken.

NURSES' HOLDING POWER (SECTION 5(4))

Purpose
To allow the detention of a patient already receiving treatment for mental disorder in hospital while a doctor is found, with a view to detaining an informal patient under Section 5.

Grounds
If it appears to the nurse that
a. the patient is suffering from mental disorder to such a degree that it is necessary for his health or safety, or for the protection of others for him to be immediately restrained from leaving the hospital; and
b. that it is not practicable to secure the immediate attendance of a practitioner for the purpose of formulating a report under Section 5(2).

Recommendations
A nurse of the prescribed class (to be laid down by Order) who must record the decision in writing and deliver it to the managers of the hospital as soon as possible.

Duration
A maximum of six hours from the time that the decision to hold the patient is recorded in writing*. The power ceases upon the arrival of the doctor having power to furnish a report under Section 5.

Discharge
The power ceases upon the arrival of the doctor authorised to act under Section 5 and the patient may leave or be discharged unless the doctor takes further powers of detention.

MEDICAL RECOMMENDATIONS AND 'APPROVED' DOCTORS (SECTION 12)

(previously Section 28, MHA 1959)

BACKGROUND

When this legislation was debated in Parliament the importance of the independence of the two doctors making medical recommendations was given particular stress. The patient is thereby protected from any possibility of collusion, influence or interference with independent clinical judgment. The two doctors are required to have personally examined the patient which means interviewing him and making a preliminary assessment before signing any documents.

PRINCIPLES

1. There are two medical recommendations required to support an application for compulsory admission to hospital under Part II of the Act, one of which must be given by a doctor approved by the Secretary of State (authority delegated to the Regional Health Authority) as having special experience in the diagnosis or treatment of mental disorder as required by Section 12 of the Act. (The 'approved doctor'.) One of the two doctors should have previous acquaintance with the patient, such as a family doctor or a consultant who has previously treated him.

> Approval is usually given to doctors by any two members of a panel of assessors appointed by a Regional Health Authority and lasts for 5 years. Some authorities have used other forms of approval such as committees or Regional Advisers. The Royal College of Psychiatrists recommends that approval should only be given to psychiatrists with at least a Diploma in Psychological Medicine or the experience required for an appointment as a hospital practitioner. Now, however, the College is pressing for higher standards; a requirement that approval should be given only to those who are trained to the level required for Membership of the Royal College of Psychiatrists. Those who have had approval renewed over many years might be required to attend refresher courses. These matters are being debated.

* There would appear to be nothing to prevent the nurse initiating a new holding power at the end of six hours if a doctor has not arrived.

2. Where two doctors are required to give medical recommendations, the documents must be signed on or before the date of the application and be given by practitioners who have examined the patient personally, either together or separately. In the latter case not more than five days must have elapsed between the days on which the separate examinations took place. This restores a principle intended in the 1959 Act which appears to have been lost in drafting the Act. The patient must be admitted to hospital within 14 days of the last doctor's medical examination.

3. Only one of the two medical recommendations may normally be given by a practitioner on the staff of the hospital to which the patient is to be admitted. There are, however, exceptions to this rule in recognition of changing patterns of medical practice since the 1959 Act was introduced and difficulties which had been found in some areas of the country in recent years in obtaining recommendations from 'approved doctors' (1978 White Paper and 1976 Consultative Document).

4. The basic principle remains that the two doctors making the recommendations should be independent of each other but some relaxation of the rules relieves difficult situations in certain circumstances. The two doctors may be on the staff of the hospital to which the patient is to be admitted if it is not a private hospital or nursing home and:

    a. it is in the best interests of the patient;

    b. compliance with the basic rule would involve a delay of more than 48 hours from the completion of the examination by the first practitioner and

    c. one of the practitioners giving the recommendations works at the hospital for less than half of the time which he is bound by contract to devote to work in the health service; and

    d. where one of these practitioners is a consultant, the other does not work at that hospital in a grade in which he is under the consultant's directions.

5. A medical recommendation cannot be given by anyone acting as the applicant, or who is a partner of the applicant, or of the other doctor making the recommendation. Nor may it be given by an assistant of the applicant, any person who received payments for the maintenance of the patient or by any person within a stated degree of relationship – but a general practitioner who is employed part-time in a hospital is not regarded as a staff member for the purpose of making a medical recommendation.

MENTAL HEALTH ACT COMMISSION: GUIDANCE

The Commission has stated (Note to Doctors; 28th September 1983) that the nominated alternate doctor (Section 5(3)) should be an experienced and senior doctor rather than an inexperienced junior doctor since a decision must be made whether or not to detain a patient who has entered hospital informally.

5 Compulsory powers in the community – guardianship (Part II)

BACKGROUND

The concept of guardianship was introduced into the 1959 Act as a result of recommendations made by the Percy Commission. The Commission considered that as far as it is possible individuals who would appear to require it should be encouraged or persuaded to accept help, advice, employment or training in the community voluntarily. It was considered that some who were unwilling because of mild or chronic forms of mental disorder might benefit by being placed in the care of a guardian. The 1959 Act gave the guardian powers of control over the patient which were, in effect, the wide general powers of a father over a child of less than 14 years of age. The Act allowed for a local social services authority or a person approved by the authority to be named as a guardian. The Commission recommended that local authorities should have a duty to accept the responsibilities of guardianship whenever there were no other suitable guardians.

Guardianship is seen as a way of protecting persons who are vulnerable because of their mental disorder from exploitation, ill-treatment or neglect and ensuring that a responsible person is empowered to make important decisions on their behalf.

The use of guardianship powers has declined over the years and local authorities have often been reluctant to assume these responsibilities. In 1978 a total of 138 mentally ill and mentally handicapped people were placed under guardianship of which only 37 were mentally ill (or psychopathic) and about three-quarters were subnormal or severely subnormal.

It was considered that the powers previously given were very wide, as well as somewhat ill-defined and out of keeping, in their paternalistic approach, with modern attitudes to the care of the mentally disordered (White Paper 1981). This might account, at least in part, for the limited use of guardianship in recent years. Alternative approaches to improve the use of a valuable provision were discussed in 1976 and 1978. It was decided that the option which received widest support, and most closely met current needs, was to introduce new specific powers to restrict the liberty of the individual only so far as it is necessary to ensure that he receives the medical treatment and social support and training that he needs. This was called the 'essential powers' approach. It is considered that this approach is a more practicable one for the guardian as well as limiting the restrictions on the liberty of the patient. The Act stresses the new purpose of guardianship in that it will now be required to be in the interest of 'the welfare' of the patient rather than 'in the interests' of the patient as it was previously (and before that, under the Mental Deficiency legislation, for the 'protection of the patient').

It should be stressed that guardianship is not to be viewed as a compulsory power in the community equivalent to the powers of compulsory admission to hospital for treatment under Section 3. The value of providing powers of this kind in the community was, in fact, considered in and outside Parliament, but rejected because of the difficulties involved in supervising treatment given compulsorily outside hospital, and the inability to provide acceptable and satisfactory sanctions in the event of the patient's failure to co-operate. A short-term 28-day guardianship order proposed to gain temporary control and avoid the need for hospitalisation was also rejected as impracticable, as it would tend to increase the range of restrictions upon individual liberty and it would introduce a concept which is quite different to the purpose of guardianship, which is to provide longer term guidance, supervision, influence and support to assist vulnerable and handicapped individuals to continue to live their lives in the community.

THE POWERS OF GUARDIANS (SECTION 8)

(previously Section 34, MHA 1959)

PRINCIPAL CHANGES

1. A guardianship application confers upon the authority, or person named as a guardian, the following powers:

   a. the power to require the patient to reside at a place specified by the authority, or person named as a guardian.
   b. the power to require the patient to attend at places, and times so specified, for the purpose of medical treatment, occupation, education or training;
   c. the power to require access to the patient to be given, at any place where the patient is residing, to any registered medical practitioner, Approved Social Worker or other person so specified.

It will be observed that these are limited but important powers, which imply associated responsibilities to be undertaken by the guardian. In specifying a required place of residence, the guardian will not only ensure that the patient is not living in unsatisfactory accommodation or sleeping rough, but he will need to take steps to find him accommodation that is suitable. Similarly, he would not simply direct the patient to attend a clinic or occupational therapy centre, but, if necessary, would ensure that he can and does find his way there. However, the guardian has no powers to give consent to treatment on behalf of the patient and the 'consent to treatment' rules do not apply.

2. Should the patient fail to co-operate and he absents himself from his residence without the guardian's permission, he may be taken into custody and be brought back. After 28 days this power to retake the patient expires for patients of all four principal categories of mental disorder (under the previous Act patients suffering from psychopathic disorder or subnormality could be taken into custody for up to six months but this difference has been removed). The patient may in certain circumstances be transferred to hospital as if an order had been made under Section 3.

3. There are no other sanctions should the patient fail to co-operate in other ways; the essential powers are thought to give sufficient authority to the guardian to allow him to influence the patient beneficially. But *Regulations* specify further 'duties' of guardians.

GUARDIANSHIP APPLICATIONS (SECTION 7)
(previously Section 33, MHA 1959)

Purpose
To place a patient who has attained the age of 16 years under the supervision of a guardian. (Local social services authority or named individual).

Grounds
1. He is suffering from mental disorder being mental illness, severe mental impairment, psychopathic disorder or mental impairment.
2. That it is necessary in the interests of the welfare of the patient or for the protection of other persons that he should be so received (into guardianship).

Medical recommendations
Two doctors (one 'approved') who have personally examined the patient, together or separately.

When they have examined the patient separately, not more than five days should have elapsed between the two examinations. The patient may be described as suffering from more than one of the forms of mental disorder referred to (see grounds above) but the doctors must both agree on at least one of them.

A medical recommendation may NOT be given by a person who is:

a. the applicant
b. a partner of the applicant or of a practitioner by whom another medical recommendation is given for the purpose of the application

   c. a person employed as an assistant by the applicant or by any such practitioner as aforesaid

   d. a person who receives or has an interest in the receipt of any payments made on account of the maintenance of the patient or

   e. the person named as a guardian in the application.

Applications

The nearest relative of the patient or an Approved Social Worker (who must consult the nearest relative if it is possible to do so). An objection from the nearest relative prevents the Approved Social Worker from making the application.

The applicant must have personally seen the patient within the previous 14 days. If the proposed guardian is not the local social services authority, the application must be accompanied by a written statement from the proposed guardian that he is willing to act as the guardian.

The guardianship application shall state the age of the patient, or, if his exact age is not known, the applicant shall state (if it be the fact) that the patient is believed to have attained the age of 16 years.

The application is sent to the local social services authority named as guardian, or the local social services authority for the area in which the person named as guardian resides, within 14 days of the last medical examination.

Duration

Six months. Unless renewed for a further six months by the Responsible Medical Officer (where the patient is subject to the guardianship of the local authority) or the nominated medical attendant in any other case (usually the family doctor). After a further six months renewal periods are at annual intervals.

Powers of discharge

The Responsible Medical Officer, the responsible social services authority or the nearest relative may discharge the patient.

The patient may appeal to a Mental Health Review Tribunal within six months of the guardianship order being made and similarly after a further six months.

There are no arrangements for automatic reviews as there are for patients detained in hospital.

Powers of transfer

If any person acting as guardian dies, or gives notice of a desire to relinquish the guardianship of the patient, the powers of guardianship shall then be vested in the local social services authority. It may then arrange for another person to accept the role of guardian. Similarly the local social services authority may take on the guardianship powers during a period of incapacity of the guardian or if a county court has ruled (upon an application from an Approved Social Worker), that the person nominated as guardian has performed his functions negligently or in a manner contrary to the interests of the welfare of the patient.

6 Applications by Approved Social Workers (Section 13)

BACKGROUND

This was previously *Section 54, MHA 1959*.

The Act lays a duty upon an Approved Social Worker to make an application for admission to hospital or for a guardianship order in respect of a person, if all the circumstances warrant it. He must have regard for the wishes of the relatives and any other factors of relevance.

PRINCIPAL CHANGES

1. The Approved Social Worker is now also required to satisfy himself that detention in a hospital is in all the circumstances of the case the most appropriate way of providing the care and medical treatment that the patient needs. The Approved Social Worker will consider the patient's present state, any previous history of hospital admission or care in the community, his relationships with his family, the wishes of relatives and patient and medical opinion. The Approved Social Worker must also consider other ways of caring for the patient, other relatives who may be able and willing to care for him, the availability of community facilities and the possibility of informal treatment, but the view of the doctors who alone can provide medical treatment must be given very careful consideration. It is not for the Approved Social Worker to assess the kind of medical treatment that might be given. In deciding against an application the Approved Social Worker must consider whether medical treatment is available elsewhere if it is needed and the ability of the doctor to continue to take responsibility for the patient's case if his recommendation for hospital care is not supported.

2. A new provision allows an Approved Social Worker to make an application outside his own social services area if this is necessary. It permits an Approved Social Worker to continue to manage the case and removes previous doubts about the authority for him to make an application outside his own locality.

Duties of Approved Social Workers
1. Application for admission to hospital in an emergency (nearest relative or Approved Social Worker).

2. Application for admission to hospital for assessment (nearest relative or Approved Social Worker).
3. Application for admission to hospital for treatment (nearest relative or Approved Social Worker who must consult the nearest relative, where practicable, and may not make an application if the nearest relative objects).
4. Similar provisions as above in connection with an application for guardianship.
5. The Approved Social Worker is required to interview the patient before making an applcation for admission to hospital, as part of his assessment, to satisfy himself that hospital admission is the most appropriate way of providing the care and medical treatment that the patient needs (see Principal Changes above).
6. If requested by the nearest relative, a local social services authority must direct an Approved Social Worker as soon as practicable to take a patient's case into consideration with a view to making an application for his admission to hospital. If the officer decides not to make an application he must inform the nearest relative of his reasons in writing.

Social work reports
A nearest relative (rather than an Approved Social Worker) may be the applicant in connection with a patient's admission to hospital compulsorily.

The managers of the hospital are then required, as soon as practicable, to give notice of that fact to the local social services authority for the patient's area so that the authority can arrange for a Social Worker to interview the patient and provide the managers with a report on his social circumstances.

7 Leave of absence; absence without leave

LEAVE OF ABSENCE FROM HOSPITAL (SECTION 17)

(previously Section 39, MHA 1959)

BACKGROUND

The Responsible Medical Officer is authorised to grant leave of absence to a detained patient subject to any necessary conditions. The patient may be required to be kept in the custody of a person on the staff of the hospital or any other authorised person. Such an arrangement might, for instance, be necessary to allow a patient to visit a sick relative, or to attend a funeral, even though his behaviour is, to some degree, unpredictable.

PRINCIPAL CHANGE

Additional authority is given in the new Act to allow any officer on the staff of another hospital to take responsibility for a patient given leave of absence in custody. This facilitates temporary transfer of a patient to another hospital for a trial period (for instance, from a secure unit to a local psychiatric hospital).

Purpose
To grant leave of absence to a patient liable to be detained in hospital.

Authority
1. The Responsible Medical Officer may grant leave of absence subject to any conditions he considers necessary in the interests of the patient or for the protection of others.
2. Leave may be granted
   a. indefinitely
   b. on specified occasions
   c. for a specific period, which may be extended in the patient's absence
   d. subject to a condition of residence at another hospital or unit.
3. If it is necessary in the interests of the patient or for the protection of others, the Responsible Medical Officer may direct that the patient is kept in the custody of another person during his absence. This may be

a. any officer on the staff of the hospital.
b. any other person authorised in writing by the managers of the hospital (e.g. a relative).
c. any officer on the staff of another hospital if the patient is required to reside in another hospital.

FAILURE TO RETURN TO HOSPITAL

If a patient fails to return from leave, if it is necessary to do so in the interests of the patient's health or for the safety of others, the Responsible Medical Officer may give notice in writing to the patient (or the person in charge of the patient) that he has decided to revoke the leave of absence and recall the patient to hospital.

EXEMPTION FROM RECALL

A patient may NOT be recalled if
a. the order authorising his detention has expired
b. if he has been continuously absent on leave for a period of six months (unless he has already returned to hospital or he is absent without leave at the end of six months).

PATIENTS ABSENT WITHOUT LEAVE

BACKGROUND

Patients who are absent without leave can be taken into custody and returned to hospital by certain authorised people. This authority cannot be exercised if a patient has remained out of hospital for a specified period of time.

PRINCIPAL CHANGES

1. Previously a patient who was classified as suffering from psychopathic disorder or subnormality and was over 21 years of age could not be taken into custody after a continuous absence of six months. Mentally ill and severely subnormal patients could not be taken into custody after a continual absence of 28 days. *The time limit of 28 days now applies to patients of all categories (and all ages*, since the age limits have been removed elsewhere in the Act).

2. Another new qualification applies to patients subject only to short-term detention (72 hours or 28 days). Such patients may not be retaken into custody if the period of detention has expired.

Purpose
To return and re-admit patients absent without leave.

Grounds
a. The patient is for the time being liable to be detained.
b. The patient·
   (i) is absent without leave having been granted by the Responsible Medical Officer.

(ii) Although leave of absence from the hospital has been granted, he has failed to return or failed to respond, having been informed that he has been recalled.

c. Where the patient is subject to guardianship and absents himself without leave of the guardian from a place at which he is required to reside.

Authority to take into custody

a. Hospital patients may be taken into custody and returned to hospital by:
  (i) any Mental Welfare Officer
  (ii) any officer on the staff of the hospital
  (iii) any constable
  (iv) any officer of a hospital to which the patient has been transferred.
  (v) any person authorised in writing by the managers of the appropriate hospital

b. Patients subject to guardianship may be taken into custody and returned to the place where they are required to reside by:
  (i) any officer on the staff of the local social services authority
  (ii) any constable
  (iii) any person authorised in writing by the guardian or a local social services authority.

Duration of authority to retake the patient

a. No person may be taken into custody and returned to hospital or to the care of a guardian after the expiration of *28 days*.

b. A patient subject to short-term detention may not be taken into custody if the period for which he is liable to detention has expired.

8 Duration of authority and renewal of compulsory powers

BACKGROUND

The Mental Health Act 1959 authorised a period of not more than one year initially as the duration of the authority to detain a patient in hospital for treatment, on a Hospital Order, or under guardianship.

This was, of course, the maximum period and the authority could be terminated if it was appropriate at any earlier time, but while the authority remained, the controls given to the Responsible Medical Officer or the guardian continued.

The time period allowed the patient one opportunity in 12 months to apply to a Mental Health Review Tribunal if he wished to appeal against the compulsory orders.

When mental health legislation was being reviewed there was general agreement that the periods of detention should be shortened and that any extension should be dependent upon a more detailed review of the patient's clinical state and the continued need to apply compulsion.

PRINCIPAL CHANGES

DURATION OF AUTHORITY (SECTION 20)

(previously Section 43, MHA 1959)
1. The duration of authority to detain the patient in hospital or to keep the patient under guardianship is now a period of six months beginning with the day on which the patient was admitted (under Section 3) or the day on which the guardianship application was accepted (under Section 7).

   2. The authority may be renewed for a further period of six months (previously one year) and for subsequent periods of one year's duration (previously two years).

   3. The Responsible Medical Officer must review the need for continued detention or guardianship after four months (initially) and then, if the patient is further detained, after 10 months, then annually thereafter.

   4. A patient (other than a patient subject to a Hospital Order) has

the right to apply to a Mental Health Review Tribunal within the first six months of detention in hospital. All patients subject to guardianship (as at present), may apply within the first six months and again in the next six months if the detention or guardianship is renewed. There are twice as many opportunities for all groups to apply to a Tribunal under the 1983 statute compared with the position under the Mental Health Act 1959.

5. If a patient admitted for treatment (or transferred from guardianship) does not exercise his right to apply to a Tribunal, the managers of the hospital must automatically refer his case after the first six months and again, should his detention continue and the patient has again not exercised his right of appeal, after three years (see Chapter 14). The six months referral does not apply to a patient subject to a Hospital Order.

RENEWAL OF COMPULSORY POWERS

Background
Previously, the Responsible Medical Officer was required to examine the patient within two months of the expiration of the period of compulsory detention. If it appeared to him that it was necessary 'in the interests of the patient's health or safety or for the protection of other persons' that the patient should continue to be liable to be detained, then he was required to report this to the managers of the hospital. This alone was sufficient information to authorise a further period of detention, but without further elaboration.

Principal change
1. Under the 1983 Act the Responsible Medical Officer is required to be satisfied that certain conditions are met to renew the authority for detention. These are substantially the same as the grounds for admission for treatment under Section 3, but in addition, one of two alternative conditions must be fulfilled in the case of mentally ill or severely mentally impaired patients.

2. Before making a report the Responsible Medical Officer must consult one or more other persons who have been concerned with the patient's treatment.

CONDITIONS FOR RENEWAL OF POWERS TO DETAIN (SECTION 20(4))
The conditions are:
a. that the patient is suffering from mental illness, severe mental impairment, psychopathic disorder or mental impairment, being a mental disorder of a nature or degree which makes it appropriate for him to receive medical treatment in a hospital; and
b. that such treatment is likely to alleviate or prevent a deterioration of his condition (but see d. below); and
c. that it is necessary for the health or safety of the patient or for the protection of other persons that he should receive such treatment and that it cannot be provided unless he continues to be detained.

d. In the case of patients suffering from *mental illness* or *severe mental impairment* an alternative condition to b. is that the patient, if discharged is unlikely to be able to care for himself, to obtain the care which he needs or to guard himself againt serious exploitation.

The conditions, therefore, ensure that the patient is suffering from one of the forms of mental disorder, that it is in all cases treatable (although on admission the treatability test only applies to psychopathic and mentally impaired patients) or alternatively for the mentally ill or severely mentally impaired, that the patient is gravely incapacitated. The necessity for *hospital* treatment is also emphasised and that detention (as opposed to informal admission) is required.

RENEWAL OF AUTHORITY FOR GUARDIANSHIP (SECTION 20(6))

The Section requires the Responsible Medical Officer (in the case of a patient who is subject to the guardianship of a local social services authority) or the patient's nominated medical practitioner (where the guardian is a private individual) to examine the patient within the two months before the guardianship order is due to expire. He will consider the need to extend the order for a second period of six months (or subsequent periods of one year). If there are grounds for continuing the order this must be reported to the guardian and to the local social services authority if it is not itself the guardian. This gives authority for continuation.

The grounds for renewal of a guardianship order are the same grounds required for making a guardianship application.

CONDITIONS FOR RENEWAL OF GUARDIANSHIP

a. the patient is suffering from mental illness, severe mental impairment, psychopathic disorder or mental impairment.
b. The mental disorder is of a nature or degree which warrants his reception into guardianship.
c. It is necessary in the interests of the welfare of the patient or for the protection of other persons that the patient should remain under guardianship.

RECLASSIFICATION

1. If the Responsible Medical Officer or nominated medical attendant after examining the patient for a report required for renewal of hospital detention or guardianship, decided that the patient is suffering from a different form of mental disorder from that given on the original application (e.g. mental illness rather than psychopathic disorder) then the application has effect as though it specified the same disorder as in the renewal report. The patient and his nearest relative should be notified. The patient in any event has a right of appeal to a Tribunal within 28 days.

2. Reclassification is important because (see above) the conditions for renewal differ according to the form of mental disorder specified. If the patient is reclassified as suffering from psychopathic disorder or mental impairment (but not mental illness or severe mental impairment) the 'treatability' test must be satisfied in addition to the other conditions supporting renewal of compulsory powers. If the treatability test does not apply (that further medical treatment in hospital is likely to alleviate or prevent a deterioration of the patient's condition) then the patient cannot be further detained.

3. A report may also be made to the managers during the period of detention or guardianship, and in all cases one or more persons concerned with the patient's treatment should be consulted before the report is made.

9 Care and treatment of detained patients

VISITING AND THE EXAMINATION OF PATIENTS (SECTION 24)

(previously Section 37, MHA 1959)

BACKGROUND

This Section gives authority to a doctor or other appropriate person to visit a patient and interview him in private in connection with functions required under the Act (for instance, in connection with a Tribunal application). This applies to hospitals and mental nursing homes.

PRINCIPAL CHANGE

1. Doctors who are required to visit a nursing home to advise the managers whether a patient should be discharged have the authority to ask to see and examine any records of the patient (not simply the medical records). This authority is now extended to the following:

   1. A visiting medical practitioner advising upon whether an application should be made to a Mental Health Review Tribunal.
   2. A doctor visiting to assess the patient's condition for the purpose of a Tribunal hearing.
   3. A doctor considering advice to the nearest relative on the power to discharge the patient.

2. Doctors authorised by the Secretary of State to visit and inspect mental nursing homes, and to examine patients in them when there has been an application to discharge a patient are authorised to examine the records of the patient. This now includes medical records, nursing records, and any other records kept by staff about patients.

RECLASSIFICATION OF PATIENTS (SECTION 16)

(previously Section 38, MHA 1959)

When a patient has been detained in hospital for treatment for some time (or has been subject to a guardianship order) the clinical team may decide that the Mental Health Act category of mental disorder used when he was first detained is incorrect. It would then be appropriate to reclassify the patient, and this Section provides for this to be done formally and gives authority to the patient, and his nearest relative, to appeal against the new classification. For instance, the patient may initially have been recorded as suffering from mental illness but his behaviour, clinical observations, tests, and perhaps his family history, might now indicate that he is suffering from psychopathic disorder.

PRINCIPAL CHANGES

1. Where a detained patient is reclassified as suffering from psychopathic disorder or mental impairment, the reclassification report must indicate that the patient is likely to benefit from treatment, otherwise the authority to detain the patient must cease.

   2. Before making a report to reclassify a patient the Responsible Medical Officer must consult one or more other members of the clinical team and subsequently record that he has done so.

   3. The reclassification arrangements are confined to patients detained in hospital for treatment (or on a guardianship order) and the consent to treatment arrangements continue to apply while a patient remains in hospital.

Purpose
To reclassify a patient detained in hospital for treatment or a patient subject to guardianship.

Grounds
1. It appears to the Responsible Medical Officer that the patient is suffering from a form of mental disorder other than the form, or forms specified in the original application.
2. The report must state the new form of mental disorder from which the patient is considered to be suffering, and that the other conditions for the continuation of detention are satisfied.
3. If the new diagnostic classification is psychopathic disorder or mental impairment, the report must include a statement of the Responsible Medical Officer's opinion whether further medical treatment in hospital is likely to alleviate, or prevent, a deterioration of the patient's condition.
4. The Responsible Medical Officer must indicate that he has consulted one or more members of the clinical team. ('Persons who have been professionally concerned with the patient's medical treatment').

Application
From the Responsible Medical Officer to the managers of the hospital, or to the guardian (who may be the local social services authority).

Duties of managers or guardian
The patient and nearest relative must be informed if the patient is reclassified. The patient must be discharged if the grounds for detention are not fulfilled.

Mental Health Review Tribunals
The patient or his nearest relative may apply to a Mental Health Review Tribunal within 28 days of being informed of the reclassification. The Mental Health Review Tribunal has the power to discharge the patient if it is appropriate. It also has a power to reclassify a patient.

10 Relatives of patients

BACKGROUND

Relatives, and particularly the 'nearest relative', have important functions and powers under the Act. The meaning of 'nearest relative' is carefully defined and listed in order of preference and includes a man or woman who has been living as a husband or wife of the patient for at least six months (but not in preference to a legal husband or wife unless there is a legal separation or genuine desertion).

When the new legislation was debated in Parliament it was decided to extend the principle behind the meaning of 'nearest relative' to include a partner in a stable, caring relationship, even if the individuals are not blood relatives but are close friends of the same or opposite sex. In these circumstances, it was argued, a close friend who has been caring for a patient might reasonably take preference over a close blood relative with whom the patient has had little contact for a long time.

PRINCIPAL CHANGES

1. The elder parent takes priority in the list of individuals who may act as the nearest relative (rather than a father always having precedence over a mother as in the previous Act).

2. However, a relative with whom the patient usually lives, or who has been caring for him, takes priority over other relatives who are listed higher in order of precedence in the Act.

3. But a person, other than a relative, with whom the patient has been living for not less than five years can be regarded as the 'nearest relative'. Such a person cannot displace a husband or wife unless there is a legal separation or genuine desertion.

4. Relatives living in the Channel Islands or the Isle of Man are not now debarred from acting as the nearest relative as they were previously. Only persons *not* ordinarily resident in the United Kingdom, Channel Islands or Isle of Man are debarred if the patient *is* ordinarily resident there. If both patient and relative ordinarily live

abroad then, in these circumstances, the relative may be the 'nearest relative' (if, for instance, they are both visiting this country when one of them becomes ill).

FUNCTIONS OF RELATIVES (SECTION 26)

1. The nearest relative may make *application*:

   a. for admission for assessment or treatment,
   b. for admission in an emergency,
   c. or guardianship.

2. The nearest relative must be *consulted*, where practicable:

Before an application for admission for treatment or for a guardianship order is made by an Approved Social Worker (who may not make it if the nearest relative objects).

3. The nearest relative must be *informed*;

When an Approved Social Worker makes an application for admission for assessment.

4. The nearest relative has the power to order the discharge of a patient detained for assessment or treatment (with certain restrictions).

5. The nearest relative may, in respect of a patient admitted on a Hospital Order, make an application to a Mental Health Review Tribunal in the second six months from the date of the order and in any subsequent period of 12 months.

6. The nearest relative must be notified if a detained patient (or a patient subject to guardianship) is reclassified. The nearest relative may apply to a Mental Health Review Tribunal within 28 days.

DEFINITION OF NEAREST RELATIVE

Relative means any of the following:

   a. husband or wife
   b. son or daughter
   c. father or mother
   d. brother or sister
   e. grandparent
   f. grandchild
   g. uncle or aunt
   h. nephew or niece

Adopted children, relatives of the half blood (e.g. half sister) and illegitimate children are all regarded as natural, legitimate children and of 'the full blood' (e.g. full sister).

Nearest relative means the first surviving person appearing in the list above, but full blood relatives take preference over half blood relatives of the same description (two brothers or two sisters) and the elder of two relatives of the same description or degree of relationship takes preference.

EXCLUSION FROM RIGHT TO ACT AS NEAREST RELATIVE

A person may *not* act as the nearest relative;

a. in the case of a patient ordinarily resident in the United Kingdom, the Channel Isles or the Isle of Man, if the relative is not ordinarily resident there;
b. if the relative is the husband or wife of the patient but is permanently separated from the patient, either by agreement or by the order of a court.
   Similarly, if the husband or wife has deserted or has been deserted by the patient for a period which has not come to an end;
c. if the relative is under 18 years of age (unless the relative is the husband, wife, father or mother of the patient);
d. if the relative is a man subject to an order removing his authority over the patient under Section 38 of the Sexual Offences Act 1956 (relating to incest with a girl under the age of 18).

PERSONS LIVING TOGETHER AS HUSBAND AND WIFE

'Husband' and 'wife' in the list defining nearest relatives above includes a person who is living with the patient as husband or wife (or who was living with the patient in that capacity before the patient entered hospital), but the relationship must have existed for a period of not less than six months. However, such a person cannot displace the rights of a legal husband or wife unless there has been a legal separation or desertion as described above.

PERSONS (OTHER THAN RELATIVES) LIVING TOGETHER

A person, other than a relative, with whom the patient has been residing for not less than five years is treated as a relative and would be placed last in the list of relatives in order of priority given earlier in this chapter. A friend cannot displace the rights of a husband or a wife of the patient unless there has been a legal separation or desertion.

CARING RELATIVE

Where a patient ordinarily lives with, or has been cared for by one or more of his relatives (as defined above) his nearest relative is determined by:

a. Giving preference to the caring relative or relatives over others in the list (noting the rights of husbands and wives).
b. Where there is more than one caring relative, one takes precedence over the other according to the principles already outlined.

It should be noted that the special consideration given to a caring relative here includes a close friend as described earlier.

DETERMINING WHO IS THE NEAREST RELATIVE

Examples

1. A student living alone in lodgings requires admission to hospital. His nearest relative is found by reference to the list above. His mother is the older of his parents, who are both living, so she is the nearest relative for the purposes of the Act.

2. An elderly man has lived with his niece for the past 10 years. Although other relatives are living, including brother and sisters, his niece is the nearest relative.

3. Two nurses are close friends and have shared a flat for 7 years. Although parents and other relatives are alive in this country, one nurse may act as nearest relative on behalf of the other.

4. Two male musicians have cohabited in a homosexual relationship for many years. Each may act as nearest relative for the other. However, one of them, although separated from his wife, is not legally separated. In his case the wife takes preference over his friend.

5. An unmarried man living alone requires admission. His parents are both dead. His sister, the elder of his two siblings, takes preference as 'nearest relative'.

CHILDREN AND YOUNG PERSONS IN CARE

In some instances, the local authority or an individual has the rights and powers of a parent. In this case the authority or person is the nearest relative in preference to anyone else, with the exception of a husband or wife of the young person, if married; and with the exception of a parent, provided that the parent is not the reason for the child being in care.

Parental rights may be vested in an authority or person by virtue of:

a. Section 3 of the Child Care Act 1980 (which relates to the assumption by the local authority of parental rights and duties in relation to a child in their care);

b. Section 10 of the Child Care Act (which relates to the powers and duties of local authorities with respect to persons committed to their care under the Childrens and Young Persons Act 1969); or

c. Section 17 of the Social Work (Scotland) Act 1968 (which makes the corresponding provision for Scotland).

NEAREST RELATIVE OF A MINOR (UNDER GUARDIANSHIP, ETC.)

1. Where a patient under the age of 18

a. is under the guardianship of a person who is not his nearest relative; or

b. is under the guardianship of two people of whom one is a relative; *then the person or persons having guardianship or custody shall be the nearest relative* in preference to anyone else. This may result from an order in respect of the guardianship of minors (including an Order under Section 38 of the Sexual Offences Act 1956) or by virtue of a deed or will executed by his father or mother.

2. Where a patient under the age of 18

is, as a result of a court order, or as a result of matrimonial proceedings, or by virtue of a separation agreement between his father and mother in the custody of one of them, *then that person is the nearest relative.*

ACTING NEAREST RELATIVE (SECTION 29)

Background

There are circumstances in which it may be necessary for a court to order that the functions of a nearest relative should be vested in another person. This might occur if the apparent nearest relative is unsuitable or no one can be clearly identified as able to take the responsibility.

This Section describes the power of a County Court to make an order, the grounds upon which it may be made, and the arrangements to discharge or vary the order.

Purpose

Power of a County Court to appoint an acting nearest relative who may be:
a. The applicant (or local social services authority if the application is made by an Approved Social Worker).
b. Any other person specified in the application.

The person appointed must be a person who, in the opinion of the Court is a proper person to act as the patient's nearest relative and is willing to do so.

Functions

The functions of the nearest relative of the patient shall be exercised by the person appointed while the order remains in force.

Grounds

a. The patient has no nearest relative or no-one can be defined or located.
b. The nearest relative of the patient is incapable of acting as such by reason of mental disorder or other illness.
c. The nearest relative unreasonably objects to making an application for hospital admission for treatment or a guardianship application.
d. The nearest relative has unreasonably exercised his power to discharge the patient from an order. ('Without due regard to the welfare of the patient or the interests of the public'.)

Applicant

a. any relative of the patient,
b. any other person with whom the patient is residing (or was residing),
c. An Approved Social Worker.

DISCHARGE (AND VARIATION) OF ORDERS MADE BY A COUNTY COURT

Discharge of an order

An order made by a County Court appointing an 'acting nearest relative' may be discharged by the court on an application:

a. by the acting nearest relative whatever the grounds upon which the order was originally made;
b. from a competent nearest relative when the order was made because a nearest relative could not be found or was not competent.

VARIATION OF AN ORDER

On the application of the acting nearest relative or an Approved Social Worker the order may be varied by substituting some other person or a local social services authority to assume the functions of nearest relative of the patient.

Duration of an order

Unless previously discharged, a County Court order ceases to have effect at the expiration of any specified period (if it had a time limit) or as follows:

a. The order lasts until the patient is discharged from hospital or guardianship if he was so detained at the time the County Court order was made (or if he became detained within three months of the order being made).
b. If he was not in hospital or under guardianship at the time the County Court order was made and did not become detained within three months, then the order lapses at the end of that period of time.

DELAYED DISCHARGE OF A DETAINED PATIENT

In the case of a patient liable to be detained for assessment, the doctor or Approved Social Worker may consider that the nearest relative's refusal to agree to any further detention is unreasonable and an application to a County Court under this Section may be started. If such an application is pending immediately before the expiration of an order admitting the patient for assessment then the order may be extended:

a. until the application to the County Court has been finally disposed of (including time to appeal).
b. If an order is made appointing an acting nearest relative then the order admitting the patient to hospital for assessment can be extended for a further *seven* days.

Duration

Where the County Court makes an order under this Section because no nearest relative is identifiable or the nearest relative is not capable of acting, then the order *may* be made for a specified period of time (unless discharged before then). The court has discretion about this.

The arrangement allows an acting nearest relative to use his authority if a discharged patient subsequently needs to be detained again. It may also be useful if it is known that a relative will become available to assume these functions at the end of a period of time.

Mental Health Review Tribunals

The nearest relative may appeal with 12 months if a new detention or guardianship order is made.

11 Mentally disordered offenders

BACKGROUND

Most people charged with a criminal offence, or convicted in a Crown Court or a Magistrates' Court, are not suffering from a significant mental disorder. Some suffer from less severe conditions which may be dealt with in prison, and some may be placed on a psychiatric probation order.

If an offender is suffering from a serious degree of mental disorder a court may consider making a Hospital Order or Guardianship Order under Section 37 of the Act, if the critieria for making an order are satisfied. A Hospital Order or Guardianship Order is not a sentence; it is an alternative disposal and the person becomes a patient not a prisoner. In hospital his status is similar in most respects to a patient admitted from the community under Section 3 for treatment. The patient is treated no differently and he may be discharged whenever it is appropriate. The doctor has no obligation to detain the patient any longer than is necessary simply because he might have received a prison sentence for his offence; and the responsibility for deciding when the patient may be discharged is his. If the court considers that the public requires protection then an order restricting discharge should be imposed at the time the order is made (see below); it is a matter for the court to decide.

Sometimes the *court* remands an accused person for medical examination while on bail or in custody to consider if a Hospital Order or Guardianship Order should be made. In other cases this is requested by a *lawyer* either representing the *defence* or the *prosecution*. If a Hospital Order is recommended, two doctors must give evidence, oral or written, but the final decision is the responsibility of the court. All the evidence must be considered to decide if a Hospital Order is in the best interests of the public and the accused individual in all the circumstances of the case. Occasionally a judge might decide not to make a Hospital Order despite receiving positive medical recommendations, but this is unusual.

A Hospital Order does not necessarily require that the patient is cared for in secure conditions, but they may be necessary. The patient can be admitted to any appropriate hospital. If the patient is thought to require treatment under conditions of special security because of his dangerous, violent or criminal propensities a doctor intending to make a recommendation to a court can apply to the Secretary of State for Social Services (for address see Appendix) requesting the admission of the patient to a Special Hospital (see page 72). In recent years, however, there have been increasing difficulties in obtaining a bed for some mentally abnormal offenders. A programme to establish secure hospital units in each N.H.S. region is now established (Bluglass 1978, Gostin 1984) but this will only go part of the way to solving the problem. Meanwhile, it is thought that the prisons contain some people who should be in hospital but the courts have been unable to make a Hospital Order in respect of many of them because they could not find an appropriate bed. The increasing availability of secure beds together with some of the new legislation described below will go some way towards easing these problems.

REMANDS TO HOSPITAL

REMAND TO HOSPITAL FOR A REPORT (SECTION 35)

Background
A Crown Court may remand a defendant at any time for medical and psychiatric reports to be obtained. The court may remand in custody for the reports to be prepared in the hospital wing of a prison, or by granting the defendant bail with a condition of residence in hospital. However, the facilities in prison are restricted, there are few opportunities for technical and specialist investigations and time is often limited. Remand to hospital on bail provides no powers to detain a disturbed defendant should he decide to leave and is sometimes inappropriate.

Magistrates' Courts may similarly remand in custody or on bail after conviction, or, if it is satisfied that a defendant accused of an imprisonable offence did the act or made the omission charged he may be remanded in custody or on bail without proceeding to a conviction (Magistrates' Courts Act 1980, Sections 10 and 30).

The Butler Report on Mentally Abnormal Offenders recommended that courts should be able to remand directly to hospital if necessary where bail is inappropriate. Such a remand implies that a suitable level of security will be available in the hospital and it is likely that the new arrangements will, in practice, be used for remands to the new secure units or to hospitals which have arranged suitably secure accommodation. Remands to prison hospitals or on bail will continue where they appear to be appropriate and the new provision is, in practice, an alternative to remand in custody.

General principles
1. The Mental Health Act 1983 gives the Crown Court or Magistrates' Court a new power to remand an accused person to a specified hospital for a medical report to be prepared (Section 35) on the evidence of a doctor.

2. The categories of 'accused person' are defined.

3. The Section describes the grounds for remanding an accused person for a report, the need to ensure that a hospital is willing to receive him, the powers given to arrange further remands if necessary and the authority to re-arrest the patient should he abscond. Other rights of the defendant are described.

4. The accused person is not remanded for treatment. He may be given treatment as if he were an informal patient but the consent to treatment provisions in the Act for *detained* patients do not apply.

Purpose

To empower a Crown Court or Magistrates' Court to remand an accused person to a specified hospital for a report to be obtained on his mental condition.

Grounds

1. In relation to a Crown Court an 'accused person' is *any* person awaiting trial (including trial for murder) who is accused of an imprisonable offence, or a person who has been convicted but not yet sentenced (but excluding persons convicted of murder).

2. In relation to a Magistrates' Court an 'accused person' is any person who has been charged with an offence punishable on summary conviction with imprisonment if the court is satisfied that he did the act or made the omission charged, or if he consents to the remand to hospital. The court may similarly remand to hospital for a report a person convicted by the court of such an offence.

3. There is reason to suspect that the accused person is suffering from mental illness, psychopathic disorder, mental impairment or severe mental impairment.

4. It would be impracticable to obtain a medical report if he were remanded on bail.

Medical recommendations

1. The court must receive written or oral evidence from *one* registered medical practitioner (*not* necessarily an 'approved' doctor).

2. The court must receive written or oral evidence from the medical practitioner who would be responsible for making the report (who may be the doctor recommending the remand) or another person representing the managers of the hospital, that arrangements have been made for his admission to the hospital within seven days of the date of the remand.

Applications

An application may be made by the defence or the prosecution for a remand or may be made by the court itself. Where an accused person has initially been remanded in custody or on bail a doctor might recommend to the court that a remand to hospital is advisable in order that a more satisfactory report may be prepared.

Duration

Initially 28 days. The remand may be renewed at 28 day intervals for up to 12 weeks if it is necessary to complete the assessment. The court may at any time terminate the remand if it appears appropriate to do so; if, for instance, it learns that the report is completed or that the person cannot be adequately assessed in hospital because of his behaviour.

Further remands

1. On the written or oral evidence of the medical practitioner responsible for making the report that a further remand is necessary for completing the assessment satisfactorily.
2. The accused person need not be present when a further remand is being considered if he is represented by Counsel or by a solicitor (in a Magistrates' Court).

Independent examination

The accused person is entitled to obtain, at his own expense, an independent report on his medical condition from a doctor of his own choosing and on the basis of it to apply to the court to have his remand terminated.

Powers of conveyance and re-arrest

1. The Section empowers a constable or any other person to take the person to hospital within seven days of the remand date and authorises the managers of the hospital to admit and detain him.
2. If the person absconds from hospital, or while being conveyed there, he may be re-arrested without warrant and must be brought back to the court that remanded him as soon as practicable. The court may then terminate the remand and deal with him in any other appropriate way or may decide to continue the remand.

NOTE: The power to remand to hospital for a report will come into force on 1st October 1984.

REMAND TO HOSPITAL FOR TREATMENT (SECTION 36)

Background

Sometimes an individual accused of an offence is suffering from a serious degree of mental disorder. Remand on bail to enable him to be admitted to hospital is often inappropriate and prison hospitals are not equipped or staffed to treat severe mental illness. The Butler Committee on Mentally Abnormal Offenders recommended that a court should be able to remand a defendant to hospital *for treatment*.

The Mental Health Act 1983 includes new powers to enable a court to make such a remand as an alternative to a remand in custody while awaiting trial. Like the power to remand for a report, this new provision implies that a suitable level of security is available at the receiving hospital or unit.

There are other provisions in the Act (Sections 47 and 48) to allow the transfer from prison to hospital of a person suffering from mental illness or severe mental impairment (sentenced or remanded in custody) who becomes in need of treatment *while in prison*.

An advantage of this form of remand is that it can be used to avoid the court finding an accused person unfit to plead, with all the unsatisfactory consequences of such a decision.

General principles

1. The Act gives a Crown Court (but not a Magistrates' Court) the power to remand an accused person to a specified hospital for treatment (Section 36) on the evidence of two doctors.

2. The categories of 'accused person' for the purpose of this Section are defined.

3. The Section describes the grounds for remanding an accused person for treatment, the need to ensure that a hospital can receive him and the powers given to arrange further remands if necessary.

4. The person is remanded *for treatment* and the consent to treatment provisions apply.

Purpose

To empower a Crown Court to remand an accused person to a specified hospital for treatment.

Grounds

1. In relation to this section an 'accused person' is any person who is in custody awaiting trial before the Crown Court for an imprisonable offence (other than murder) or who, during the course of a trial, but before sentence, is in custody for such an offence.

2. The person is suffering from *mental illness* or *severe mental impairment* of a nature or degree which makes it appropriate for him to be detained in hospital for treatment.

Medical recommendations

1. The court must receive the written or oral evidence of *two* medical practitioners (one of them an 'approved' doctor).

2. The court must receive written or oral evidence from the medical practitioner who would be in charge of the treatment (who may be one of the two recommending doctors) or some other person representing the managers of the hospital, that arrangements have been made for his admission to hospital within seven days beginning with the date of remand.

Applications

May be made by the defence or the prosecution to the court or at the request of the court. The procedure may be initiated by a prison medical officer during the course of a remand in custody.

Duration

Initially 28 days. The remand may be renewed at 28 day intervals for up to 12 weeks. The court may terminate the remand at any time if it appears appropriate to do so, for instance, the person has recovered or no effective treatment can be given.

Further remands

1. On the written or oral evidence of the Responsible Medical Officer that a further remand is warranted.

2. The accused person need not be present if he has legal representation.

Independent examination

The accused person is entitled to obtain at his own expense an independent report on his mental condition from a medical practitioner of his own choosing and on the basis of it to apply to the court to have his remand terminated (when he might return to prison).

Powers of conveyance and re-arrest

The same powers apply to this section as apply in the case of a person remanded for a report (see above).

NOTE: The power to remand to hospital for treatment will come into operation on 1st October 1984.

THE POWER TO MAKE A HOSPITAL OR GUARDIANSHIP ORDER (SECTION 37)

Principal changes

1. It is made clear that the power of a Crown Court to make a Hospital Order is confined to offences punishable with imprisonment (rather than 'any offence', as previously), with the exception of an offence for which the sentence is fixed by law (murder). It is not considered appropriate for a court to be able to order the detention in hospital of a person who has committed a minor offence which would not be punishable by imprisonment. (This has happened on some occasions in the past.)

2. The conditions for making a Hospital Order have been reformulated along similar lines to Section 3 (admission for treatment). There is a difference, however, reflected in the wording in this section. In Section 3 the considerations are:
   a. whether the patient needs treatment in hospital; and
   b. whether compulsory powers are required.

Here, the question is whether the mental disorder and all the circumstances justify a hospital order rather than any alternative disposal.

3. There is now a further condition. If the patient is suffering from *mental impairment* or *psychopathic disorder*, it must be stated that the medical treatment is likely to *alleviate or prevent a deterioration of the patient's condition*. This does not necessarily mean that the treatment will cure the condition. It means that care, or nursing or certain forms of therapy, for instance, might stabilise the patient or maintain a maximum level of functioning.

4. A Guardianship Order cannot be made by a court if the offender is under the age of 16. In fact it has been rarely used for children of this age and legislation for the care or supervision of children (Child Care Act 1980, Childrens and Young Persons Act 1969) is more appropriate. Between the ages of 16 and 17 either legislation may be used according to the best interests of the child.

5. Before making a Hospital Order the court must be satisfied that arrangements have been made for the admission of an offender to hospital. It will now be necessary for one of the doctors giving written

or oral evidence to be the medical practitioner who would be in charge of the patient's treatment (or another person may appear before the court representing the managers of the hospital). This witness can of course be additional to the two doctors giving evidence of the need for a Hospital Order. The arrangement also gives the hospital an opportunity to comment on a proposal to add a restriction order and to explain any objections that it may have, but the final decision remains the prerogative of the judge.

6. A patient admitted under a hospital order is subject to the consent to treatment requirements in Part IV of the Act.

Purpose
To empower a court to order hospital admission or the reception of the patient into guardianship (Section 37).

Grounds
1. The person has been convicted before a Crown Court of an offence punishable by imprisonment (other than an offence for which the sentence is fixed by law) or has been convicted by a Magistrates' Court of an offence punishable on summary conviction with imprisonment.
2. The offender is suffering from mental illness, psychopathic disorder, severe mental impairment or mental impairment.
3. The mental disorder is of a nature or degree which makes it appropriate for him to be detained in hospital for medical treatment and, in the case of psychopathic disorder or mental impairment, that such treatment is likely to alleviate or prevent a deterioration of his condition.
4. In the case of an offender who has attained the age of 16 years, that the mental disorder is of a nature or degree which warrants his reception into guardianship under the Act.
5. The court is of the opinion, having regard to all the circumstances, including the nature of the offence and the character and antecedents of the offender, and to the other available methods of dealing with him; that the most suitable method of disposing of the case is by means of an order under this section.

Medical recommendations
The court must receive written or oral evidence from *two* medical practitioners. At least one must be an 'approved' doctor as described in Section 12 of the Act. The form or forms of mental disorder must be specified, and the two doctors must agree that the person is suffering from at least one of the forms of mental disorder, although one of them might also refer to another category.

The court must be satisfied that arrangements have been made for the admission of the offender to a specific hospital and written or oral evidence must be provided by the doctor who would be in charge of the treatment or some other person representing the managers of the hospital.

Applications
Evidence may be called by the defence or prosecution or be requested by the court.

Duration
Six months unless renewed for a further six months and then at annual intervals.

Pending admission to hospital
If a bed is not immediately available to admit the patient on a Hospital Order the court may order that the patient is detained in a *place of safety* for up to 28 days (Section 37(4)). The patient must be admitted to hospital within this period of time or the order lapses. If it becomes impracticable to admit him to the hospital specified in the order, the Secretary of State may direct that another hospital admits him and that those having custody of the patient are informed. A 'place of safety' is usually a prison and the patient will be detained in the hospital wing.

Magistrates' court
1. Where a person is charged with an imprisonable offence before a Magistrates' Court and the court is satisfied on the evidence before it that he did the act or made the omission alleged, then a Hospital or Guardianship Order may be made *without convicting the accused* if he is suffering from mental illness or severe mental impairment justifying an order. Oral or written evidence must be received from two doctors, as above, together with evidence from the hospital that a bed is available.
No record of conviction for the offence will be recorded in criminal records.
The patient's status and rights will be as for a convicted offender on a Hospital or Guardianship Order.
2. A Magistrates' Court may also make a Hospital Order in respect of a *convicted offender*. It has no power to make an order restricting discharge, if this might be necessary, but the Court may direct the patient to be admitted to a specific hospital so that treatment may commence, and until he can have his case dealt with by a Crown Court and the need for a restriction order considered. The court may not make these arrangements unless it is satisfied by receiving written or oral evidence from the medical practitioner who would be in charge of the patient's treatment (or some other person representing the managers of the hospital) that a bed is available and the patient can be received. An order of this kind (Section 44) has the effect of a Hospital Order with an order restricting discharge until the Crown Court decides whether or not to formalise the restriction order.

POWERS OF DISCHARGE AND APPEAL

1. The patient may be discharged from a Hospital Order by the Responsible Medical Officer at any time. The nearest relative may not discharge the patient but the patient or the nearest relative may make an application to a Mental Health Review Tribunal in the period between the expiration of six months and the expiration of 12 months, beginning with the date of the order; and in any subsequent period of 12 months.
2. Patients placed under a Guardianship Order may make an application to a Mental Health Review Tribunal within the first six months of the order being made. The nearest relative of the patient may apply within the period of 12 months beginning with the date of the order and in any subsequent period of 12 months.

3. Should the patient appeal successfully against conviction any order made ceases to have affect.

RESTRICTION ORDERS

1. When a Crown Court (but not a Magistrates' Court) decides to make a Hospital Order it may go on to consider adding a further order (a restriction order) with respect to the restriction of eventual discharge of the patient from hospital.

If it appears to the court, having considered the nature of the offence, the antecedents of the offender and the risk of his committing further offences if released, that *it is necessary to protect the public from serious harm*, then the order may be made, to remain in force for an unlimited period of time or for a specified period. The decision to make a restriction order is the responsibility of the judge who is the final arbiter on the potential dangerousness of the patient, but he must first receive oral evidence from one of the two doctors making the recommendations (and preferably the receiving doctor) giving him an opportunity to comment on the proposal to make a restriction order. If he considers it is necessary, the judge may add a restriction order despite the doctor's objections.

2. During the period that a restriction order is in force, the Responsible Medical Officer is required at intervals, not exceeding one year, to examine and report to the Secretary of State on the case.*

EFFECT OF A RESTRICTION ORDER

1. The patient cannot be given leave of absence from the hospital, be transferred elsewhere, or be discharged by the Responsible Medical Officer, without the consent of the Secretary of State (Home Secretary).

2. If leave of absence is given, the Responsible Medical Officer and the Secretary of State have the power to recall the patient, take him into custody or return him to hospital, if this should be necessary.

3. The Secretary of State may remove these restrictions if he considers that they are no longer required to protect the public from serious harm. Should the Hospital Order without restrictions remain in force, it will have the same effect as in the case of a patient who was subject to a simple Hospital Order from the outset.

4. The Secretary of State may at any time discharge the patient absolutely or subject to conditions. For instance, the patient may be required to live at an agreed address, submit to the supervision of a probation officer or attend a psychiatrist periodically. Such conditions are routinely applied and are generally terminated at the end of about five years.

However, a conditionally discharged patient may be recalled at any time by warrant while the restriction order remains in force and if it is considered necessary because of a deterioration in the patient's condition, a change in his behaviour or other justifiable reasons. The Home Secretary is then required to refer the case to a Mental Health Review Tribunal within one month of his return (see below).

*It should be noted that there is no provision, either in the 1959 Act, or the 1983 Act, for the renewal of detention or reclassification of a restricted patient.

RESTRICTION ORDERS AND THE RESPONSIBLE MEDICAL OFFICER

The purpose of a restriction order applied by a Crown Court is to 'protect the public from serious harm' by delegating decisions about the patient's movements and freedom to the Home Secretary whose first concern and responsibility is the public interest. There is no statutory requirement to provide a particular level of security but clearly medical and nursing staff will make a decision in each case about their ability to obtain the patient's co-operation and control his activities. When a Hospital Order is contemplated, but there is also a probability that the court will be considering a restriction order, the doctor giving evidence on behalf of the hospital should ensure that the court fully understands the views of medical and nursing staff and the facilities (including any security) that are available.

Although a substantial number of restricted patients will be cared for in a special hospital there are many that can be managed without difficulty in local N.H.S. psychiatric hospitals and not all patients require the same level of secure provision. Some will be transferred to local hospitals after an initial period in a special hospital or secure unit.

When the Responsible Medical Officer considers that the patient is ready for leave, or one of the forms of discharge, he must contact C3 Division of the Home Office which is administratively responsible to the Home Secretary for restricted patients. The officials are invariably helpful, can be contacted by telephone (see Appendix for address and telephone number) and will readily discuss a particular case.

RIGHTS OF RESTRICTED PATIENTS TO APPLY TO A MENTAL HEALTH REVIEW TRIBUNAL

Background

Previously a restricted patient could only request the Home Secretary to refer his case to a Mental Health Review Tribunal but he could not apply directly to it himself. Further, the Mental Health Review Tribunal only had an *advisory* function, to advise the Home Secretary if he should consider discharging the patient. He would sometimes continue to detain a restricted patient, with his responsibility for the protection of the public in mind, if he considered there might be a risk if the patient was released, even though the patient's mental state did not justify it. In making up his mind, the Home Secretary is advised by the Advisory Board for Restricted Patients (Aarvold Committee) when the decision involves a patient who has been thought to be potentially dangerous. This Board was established following the recommendations of a committee chaired by Sir Carl Aarvold (Home Office 1973) following the case of Graham Young, a released Broadmoor patient. The Board is independent of the Tribunal and is concerned with advising the Home Secretary about the potential risk to the public of releasing a restricted patient: it is not concerned with the individual's rights. In practice the Board only considers cases at the request of the Home Secretary and after he has received a positive recommendation for discharge from the Responsible Medical Officer or the Mental Health Review Tribunal.

Recently the law existing under the Mental Health Act 1959 was challenged in the European Court of Human Rights in the case of X v the United Kingdom and the Court concluded that the United Kingdom was in breach of Article 5(4) of the European Convention on Human Rights. This provides that:

'Everyone who is deprived of his liberty by arrest or detention shall be entitled to take proceedings by which the lawfulness of his detention shall be decided speedily by a court and his release ordered if the detention is not lawful'.

The Court found that in England an applicant did not have this right and stated that the only basis for continuing to detain a person on the grounds of mental ill-health was continuing mental disorder. As this may change in degree it must be subject to periodic review by a court capable of ordering discharge. The law has, therefore, been changed to bring it in line with the European Convention on Human Rights (see Chapter 15, Discharge of Restricted Patients). For a detailed commentary on the European Court decision and its implications see also Walker 1982 and Gostin 1982.

Principal changes
1. A restricted patient may apply directly to a Mental Health Review Tribunal

    a. in the period between the expiration of six months and the expiration of twelve months beginning with the date of the Hospital Order with restrictions being made; and
    b. in any subsequent period of 12 months.

2. The Home Secretary may refer the case to a Mental Health Review Tribunal at any time.

3. The Home Secretary must refer to a Tribunal the case of any restricted patient who has not been reviewed by a Tribunal within the last three years. (The Tribunal will be able to consult the Aarvold Committee indirectly; through the Home Office.)

4. To give Tribunals a higher judicial status for restricted patients, as required by the European Convention, the Chairman will be a Circuit Judge or a lawyer of equivalent standing. The detailed powers given to Tribunals with reference to restricted patients are discussed in Chapter 15.

APPEALS AGAINST COURT ORDERS

APPEAL AGAINST HOSPITAL OR GUARDIANSHIP ORDER

1. If a Magistrates' Court makes a Hospital Order without recording a conviction, the patient may appeal to a Crown Court against the order,

as if it had been made on a conviction. The Crown Court retries the case and may uphold the decision to make the Hospital Order or may make another decision. The Court may send the case back to the Magistrates.

2. An appeal against a Hospital Order or Guardianship Order made in a Crown Court is made by submitting a stated case to the Divisional Court of the Queen's Bench Division.

APPEAL AGAINST A RESTRICTION ORDER

The person may appeal to the Court of Appeal (Criminal Division) which may remove the restriction order. It may also reconsider, or remove the Hospital Order and substitute a sentence, or make any other decision.

INTERIM HOSPITAL ORDERS (SECTION 38)*

Background

In the past doctors have sometimes been uncertain about the patient's likely response to treatment, or his ability to co-operate reasonably in hospital, particularly an open-door psychiatric hospital, if a Hospital Order was made. A decision has often had to be taken after one or two relatively brief interviews with the patient and mistakes can be made. Occasionally, a patient who initially appeared to have a good prospect of benefit from treatment has subsequently been found, after a period of observation, to have a concurrent instability of personality which makes his care and management difficult, or even impossible. The ability to remand a person to hospital for report or treatment will improve the quality of the doctor's assessment of the value of a Hospital Order, but these forms of remand are for a specific and limited purpose. It is often impossible to predict how the patient will react to treatment under the conditions of a Hospital Order. This is particularly important in the case of an offender suffering from psychopathic disorder, or mental impairment, when the doctor must give his opinion whether the medical treatment is likely to alleviate or prevent a deterioration of his condition.

The Butler Committee on Mentally Abnormal Offenders, following a suggestion put to it by the forensic psychiatrists who gave evidence, recommended that it would be valuable if courts were given powers to make an 'interim hospital order' committing the defendant to a specified hospital for a limited period of time for diagnosis, assessment and treatment. This would allow the doctor to assess more accurately the likely value of a Hospital Order under Section 37 and provide a more confident prognosis. Alternatively, the court might be advised that a Hospital Order is not the best way of

* To come into operation on 1st October 1984.

managing the case and alternative suggestions might be made to assist it in deciding upon the most appropriate disposal.

General principles

1. The Act gives courts the power to make an *interim hospital order* to a specified hospital for a limited period of time.

2. The grounds for making the order are specified together with the requirements as to evidence, renewal of the order and arrangements for terminating it.

3. The court may subsequently make a Hospital Order or deal with the patient in some other way.

4. The consent to treatment arrangements apply to patients detained on an interim hospital order.

Purpose
To empower a Crown Court or a Magistrates' Court to make an *interim Hospital Order* (Section 38).

Grounds
1. The person has been convicted before a Crown Court of an offence punishable by imprisonment (other than murder) or has been convicted before a Magistrates' Court of an offence punishable on summary conviction with imprisonment.
2. The offender is suffering from mental illness, psychopathic disorder, mental impairment or severe mental impairment.
3. There is reason to suppose that the mental disorder from which the offender is suffering is such that it may be appropriate for a Hospital Order to be made.

Medical recommendations
1. The written or oral evidence of two medical practitioners. At least one must be an 'approved' doctor and at least one shall be employed at the hospital specified in the order.
2. The court must receive written or oral evidence from the medical practitioner who would be in charge of the patient's treatment (or some other person representing the managers of the hospital) that arrangements have been made at the hospital for the patient's admission within a period of *28 days* from the date of the order being made. The doctor referred to may be one of the doctors making the recommendations.

Evidence
Evidence may be called by one or other side or be requested by the court.

Duration
For such period not exceeding *12 weeks* as may be specified by the Court. The order may be renewed for further periods of not more than 28 days at a time with a limit of *six months* duration.

Further remands
On the written or oral evidence of the Responsible Medical Officer. The

court may subsequently decide to make a Hospital Order or deal with the offender in some other way. The offender need not be brought before the court for the purpose of renewing the order or for a Hospital Order to be made if he is legally represented in court.

Powers of conveyance
These are the same as for remands for treatment or report (see above).

Application to tribunal
There is no right of access to a Mental Health Review Tribunal. A patient placed on a definitive Hospital Order may not make an application until six months have passed.

AVAILABILITY OF HOSPITAL CARE

INFORMATION AS TO HOSPITALS (SECTION 39)

Where a court is considering making a Hospital Order or an Interim Hospital Order, it may request:

a. the Regional Health Authority for the region in which the person resides or last resided; or
b. any other Regional Health Authority that appears to the court to be appropriate, to give information about the hospital facilities in the Region at which arrangements for the admission of a patient could be made.

In Wales the Secretary of State or his representative is responsible for providing this information.

TRANSFER TO HOSPITAL OF A SENTENCED PRISONER (SECTION 47)

(previously Section 72, MHA 1959)

Background
There are no powers to transfer a patient on a Hospital Order to prison; he is outside the penal system once the court has decided that hospital treatment is justified. But a prisoner who is serving a sentence may need psychiatric treatment because of an exacerbation or new development of mental disorder while he is in prison. Minor conditions can be managed by the prison medical officer, but the hospital wing does not have the facilities or staffing of a psychiatric hospital and patients may not be treated compulsorily and without their consent. Very urgent and serious cases have occasionally been transferred to a hospital on the medical officer's advice and with the agreement of the receiving hospital by the authority of the Prison Governor. Such arrangements are more often used to deal with urgent physical illness such as appendicitis and the patient remains in technical custody, often chaperoned throughout by a prison officer.

A patient suffering from serious mental disorder may be transferred to hospital by the Home Secretary on medical advice.

Principal changes
1. The grounds justifying transfer of a sentenced prisoner are redefined to conform with the principles established in other parts of the Act.

2. A person who recovered from his mental disorder as a result of hospital treatment was previously liable to be returned to prison up to the time when his sentence would have ended if he had received remission. Prisoners serving a fixed sentence of imprisonment can usually anticipate remission of up to one-third of their sentence for good conduct. Now, any restrictions on discharge will also cease at this time. (They previously remained in force to the end of longest period of sentence.)

3. The Home Secretary may return the person to prison if he recovers or if advised at any time that no further effective treatment or management is possible.

4. The consent to treatment provisions apply to patients transferred from prison under Section 47.

Purpose
To transfer a person serving a sentence of imprisonment to a hospital (not being a nursing home) so that he may be detained for medical treatment. Such a transfer is made by warrant of the Secretary of State and a direction made under this Section is known as a *'transfer direction'*.

Sentenced prisoners
In this Part of the Act a person serving a sentence of imprisonment means:

  a. a person detained as a result of a sentence or order for detention made by a Court in criminal proceedings (apart from an order detaining a person during Her Majesty's Pleasure).
  b. a person committed in custody under Section 115(3) of the Magistrates Courts' Act 1980 (which relates to persons who fail to comply with an order to enter into recognisances to keep the peace or be of good behaviour); and
  c. a person committed by a court to a prison or other institution to which the Prison Act 1952 applies in default of payment of any sum adjudged to be paid on his conviction.

Grounds
1. The person is suffering from mental illness, psychopathic disorder, mental impairment or severe mental impairment.
2. The mental disorder is of a nature or degree which makes it appropriate for him to be detained in a hospital for medical treatment.
3. In the case of psychopathic disorder or mental impairment, the treatment is likely to alleviate or prevent a deterioration of the patient's condition.
4. The Secretary of State (Home Secretary) is of the opinion, having regard to the public interest and all the circumstances, that the person's transfer is expedient.

Medical recommendations

The Home Secretary must receive reports from two doctors and at least one of them must be an 'approved' doctor (the other might be the prison medical officer). The two doctors must agree that the patient is suffering from one of the forms of mental disorder specified (although one of them might also mention another form of disorder).

Applications

Usually made by the prison medical officer initiating the transfer. The person must be transferred within 14 days of the order being made or the transfer direction must lapse.

Restriction directions

(Section 49) The Home Secretary may, at his discretion, add a 'restriction direction' so that the person is subject to the special restrictions set out in relation to a Hospital Order (p. 59).

Duration

1. If the Home Secretary is notified by the Responsible Medical Officer, any other doctor or a Mental Health Review Tribunal, at any time before the end of his sentence, that the patient no longer requires treatment or no further *effective* treatment can be given; then
a. he may be ordered back to a prison.
b. any power of releasing him on licence or discharging him under supervision which would have been possible if he were in prison may be exercised.
2. At the date at which his sentence would expire (with full remission) the restriction order will lapse and the patient's status is that of a patient on a hospital order (unless discharged). He may subsequently be discharged by the Responsible Medical Officer or a Mental Health Review Tribunal.

NOTE: The person's sentence is treated as having expired at the date when he would have expected to be released had he received full remission of his sentence (usually one-third unless part or all has been forfeited).

Application to a mental health review tribunal

A person transferred from prison to hospital (without a restriction order) has the right of application to a Mental Health Review Tribunal within the first six months. Those subject to a restriction direction may also make an application in the first six months of transfer to hospital, and during each subsequent period of detention.

TRANSFER TO HOSPITAL OF OTHER PRISONERS (SECTION 48)

(Previously Section 73, MHA 1959)

Background

Prisoners, other than those serving a sentence may also be transferred to hospital by the Home Secretary if he considers it justified because they are now suffering from defined forms of mental disorder. This applies to several categories of prisoner.

Principal changes

1. The grounds justifying transfer to hospital from prison of this group of prisoners have been redefined.

2. The categories of prisoner to which this section applies have been redefined.

3. The re-wording stresses that the prisoner must be in 'urgent need' of hospital treatment which the prison cannot provide.

4. The consent to treatment provisions apply.

Purpose

To authorise transfer of other prisoners from prison to hospital under a 'transfer direction' by warrant of the Secretary of State.

Grounds

1. This section applies to the following categories of prisoner:
a. Persons detained in a prison or remand centre, not being persons serving a sentence of imprisonment.
b. Persons remanded in custody by a Magistrates' Court.
c. Civil prisoners committed by a court to prison for a limited term.
d. Persons detained under the Immigration Act 1971 (pending deportation).
2. The person is suffering from mental illness or severe mental impairment (not any other form of mental disorder).
3. The mental disorder is of a nature or degree which makes it appropriate for the patient to be detained in a hospital for medical treatment and that the patient is in urgent need of such treatment.

Medical recommendations

The Home Secretary must receive reports from two doctors (at least one of them an 'approved' doctor) and the other might be a prison medical officer. The two doctors must agree that the patient is suffering from one of the two forms of mental disorder under this section.

Applications

Usually made by the prison medical officer. The person must be transferred within 14 days of the order being made.

Restriction directions

A restriction order may be made as described for sentenced prisoners above (p. 66). It is mandatory for categories a. and b. above, but discretionary for categories c. and d.

Duration

1. The order to hospital will cease with respect to persons who had been committed for trial, or remanded for sentence when the court deals with the case, although the court may make a Hospital Order.
2. The order will cease if the Home Secretary is notified by the Responsible Medical Officer, any other doctor or a Mental Health Review Tribunal at any time before the person's case is disposed of by the court, that the patient no longer requires treatment for mental disorder or that no *effective* treatment for his disorder can be given at the hospital to which he has been removed.

Application to a mental health review tribunal

A person transferred under this Section has the right of immediate appeal to a Mental Health Review Tribunal.

CIVIL PRISONERS AND PERSONS DETAINED UNDER THE IMMIGRATION ACT 1971

1. Civil prisoners, persons committed by a court to prison for a limited term (not being a prisoner convicted of a criminal offence) and, those detained under the Immigration Act 1971 shall *not* be subject to further detention in hospital resulting from a transfer direction, on the expiration of the period during which they would have been liable to be kept in custody.

2. When a transfer direction together with a restriction order have been made for either of these two categories then, if the Secretary of State is notified that:

    a. the person no longer requires treatment in hospital; or

    b. no effective treatment can be given in a specified hospital;

then the Secretary of State may by warrant direct the patient back to the prison or other place where his detention will continue.

3. The following may provide the Secretary of State with this information at any time before the expiration of the period during which the person is liable to be kept in custody.

    1. The Responsible Medical Officer.

    2. Any other medical practitioner.

    3. A Mental Health Review Tribunal.

ADMISSION TO HOSPITAL UNDER OTHER LEGISLATION

The Criminal Procedure (Insanity) Act 1964 (Section 5(1)) empowers a Court to order that an accused person is admitted to a hospital specified by the Secretary of State (Home Secretary) in the following circumstances:

    a. when a *special verdict* has been returned;

    b. when, in an appeal against conviction for an offence, the Court of Appeal are of the opinion that the proper verdict would have been a special verdict;

    c. when a court finds that the accused is *'under disability'*; or

    d. when, on an appeal against conviction, or against a special verdict, the Court of Appeal consider that the accused was *'under disability'*.

THE SPECIAL VERDICT

It was recognised for centuries that if a person was so mentally disordered at the time that he committed an unlawful act that it was unreasonable to impute guilt to him, he ought not to be held liable to conviction and punishment. The Criminal Lunatics Act 1800 first made statutory provision for a special verdict of 'not guilty on account of insanity' and following various changes in the law the Criminal Procedure (Insanity) Act 1964 restored a similar finding, a *special verdict* of 'not guilty by reason of insanity'. This means that although the accused may have committed the alleged act, he was not criminally responsible for his actions at the time. The criteria a jury must apply in arriving at this conclusion are the M'Naghten Rules (see Report of the Committee on Mentally Abnormal Offenders).

UNDER DISABILITY

Where a defendant's mental condition is such that he is not fit to be tried, he is said to be 'unfit to plead'. Such a person is usually suffering from a substantial degree of mental disorder (although very occasionally he is a deaf mute). The question as to whether the accused is 'under disability' to the extent that it would constitute a bar to his being tried by a court is a matter that is decided by an independent jury having received medical evidence.

The criteria to be applied have been established by the common law (see Butler Report).

EFFECT OF COURT ORDERS FOR ADMISSION OF SPECIAL CASES TO HOSPITAL

1. A court order in respect of a person subject to a special verdict or under disability, empowers a person authorised by the Home Secretary to convey the patient to a hospital specified by the Home Secretary within two months. Usually it is the local prison medical officer who negotiates to find a bed, on behalf of the Home Secretary, during this period, or the officials of the Home Office, itself.

2. The court may order that the patient is kept in a 'place of safety' usually the local prison hospital until a bed is found.

3. A patient admitted to hospital in these circumstances is treated as if he were a restricted hospital order patient (without limit of time).

4. The Home Secretary may remove the restrictions at a future date.

5. The patient may apply to a Mental Health Review Tribunal within the period of six months beginning with the date of the order directing him to hospital and his case must be automatically referred for review after six months. (This only applies to offender patients.)

6. The consent to treatment provisions apply.

WRITTEN MEDICAL REPORTS FOR COURTS

1. Where a court may act on a written medical report or a report from a person representing the hospital managers, for the purposes of one of the Sections of the Mental Health Act 1983 which is concerned with offenders, the report may be accepted without proof of signature or of qualifications, but the signatory of the report may be called to give oral evidence.

2. When a report is made at the request of the court (not the defence) then:

    a. a copy of the report must be given to the patient's counsel or solicitor if he has one;

    b. if unrepresented the substance of the report shall be disclosed to him;

    c. if he is a child or young person, the substance of the report shall be disclosed to his parent or guardian if present in court (or to his legal adviser if he has one);

    d. the subject of the report may require the signatory to be called to give oral evidence (except where the report relates only to arrangements for his admission to hospital). The patient may call evidence in rebuttal of the evidence in the report.

MENTAL CONDITION OF PERSONS ACCUSED OF MURDER (ON BAIL)

Background

The Mental Health Act 1983 allows persons accused of murder to be remanded to hospital for a report to be made (see page 52). Sometimes such individuals are not considered to be of any further danger to others and bail may be justified. Examples are a mother accused of killing her baby, or compassionate murders of seriously ill relatives. To improve the arrangements for bail the Bail Act 1976 has been amended to ensure that arrangements to obtain medical reports on bail are made.

Principal change

The court granting bail to a person accused or murder shall (unless satisfactory psychiatric reports have already been obtained) impose as conditions of bail:

    a. a requirement that the accused shall undergo examination by two medical practitioners for the purpose of reports (at least one 'approved' under the Act);

    b. a requirement that he shall attend such an institution or place as the court shall direct and as required by either doctor.

PERSONS IN CUSTODY DURING HER MAJESTY'S PLEASURE

1. Under certain enactments, a person may be ordered to be kept in custody during Her Majesty's Pleasure, or until the directions of Her Majesty are known. If such an individual requires hospital treatment the Secretary of State may direct that such a person is detained in a specified hospital (but not a mental nursing home). Directions may be made for transfer to a hospital.

2. The enactments concerned are:

    i. Section 16 of the Courts Martial (Appeals) Act 1968

    ii. Section 116 of the Army Act 1955

    iii. Section 116 of the Air Force Act 1955

    iv. Section 63 of the Naval Discipline Act 1957.

3. An order has the same effect as a Hospital Order with a restriction order (without limit of time).

REFERENCES

Bluglass R 1978 Regional Secure Units and Interim Security for Psychiatric Patients British Medical Journal 1 489–493

Gostin L O 1982 Human rights, judicial review and the mentally disordered offender Criminal Law Review 779–793

Gostin L O 1984 In press

Home Office 1973 Report on the review of procedures for the discharge and supervision of psychiatric patients subject to special restrictions (Aarvold Committee) Cmnd 5191 London HMSO

Home Office DHSS 1975 Report of the Committee on Mentally Abnormal Offenders Cmnd 6244 HMSO London (Butler Report)

Walker N 1982 X v The United Kingdom British Journal of Criminology 22 315–317

PRACTICE NOTE

In a judgment (delivered 9th June 1983) in the Court of Appeal, Lord Justice Lawton said that from the provisions of the National Health Service Act 1946 and the Mental Health Act 1959, it was clear that it was for doctors to decide who should be admitted to a mental hospital. Once a Hospital Order has been made by a court anyone who obstructed the execution of that order or counselled or procured others to obstruction might be guilty of contempt of court. (Regina v Harding (Bernard)) (Times' Law Reports, June 15 1983). It is therefore important for staff to be in agreement before a doctor makes a recommendation for a Hospital Order to a court.

12 Special hospitals and units

BACKGROUND

Under the National Health Service Act 1977 (Section 4) the Secretary of State is required to provide 'such institutions as appear to him to be necessary' *for persons subject to detention* under the Mental Health Act who, in the opinion of the Minister, require treatment under conditions of special security on account of their dangerous, violent or criminal propensities.

The institutions which have this function are Broadmoor Hospital, Rampton Hospital, Moss Side Hospital and Park Lane Hospital. They are known as *Special Hospitals.* They are under the direct control and management of the Secretary of State and are not subject to local administration by way of a District or Regional Health Authority. However, Rampton Hospital is managed *pro tem* by a special health authority, the Rampton Review Board, on behalf of the Secretary of State.

The Secretary of State is responsible for deciding whether or not a patient requires treatment in conditions of special security and his responsibilities in this respect and for the general management of the Special Hospitals are delegated to a group of civil servants, including doctors: the Special Hospitals Office Committee. Before a recommendation can be made to a court that a patient might be sent to a Special Hospital, an application with full clinical and offence details must be sent to the appropriate official and an offer of a Special Hospital bed must be made on the Secretary of State's behalf. The Special Hospital consultants are always very willing to discuss potential cases and will frequently examine patients to lend their support for an application for a Special Hospital bed if they consider it appropriate, or to give advice. If it is considered that, although a Hospital Order is indicated, conditions of special security are not justified, it is expected that local regions or districts will be able to provide the care needed.

The Secretary of State may transfer patients between one Special Hospital and another, or to a hospital which is not a Special Hospital (Section 123).

Broadmoor Hospital (Crowthorne, Berkshire)

Broadmoor is the oldest of the four Special Hospitals and was opened in 1863. It was initially run by the Home Office as a Criminal Lunatic Asylum. In 1949 the ownership of Broadmoor was transferred from the Home Office to the Ministry of Health and its management taken over by the Board of Control. This hospital admits mentally ill patients and those suffering from psychopathic disorder. It does not usually admit patients suffering from mental impairment.

Rampton Hospital (Retford, Nottinghamshire)

Rampton is the next oldest of the Special Hospitals. It began in 1912 as a Criminal Lunatic Asylum like Broadmoor. In 1919 responsibility was transferred from the Home Office to the Board of Control and in 1920 it became a State institution for mental defectives with dangerous or violent propensities, run by the Board of Control. In 1947 ownership was transferred to the Ministry of Health under the provisions of the National Health Service Act 1946 but the hospital continued to be managed by the Board of Control.

Rampton takes patients suffering from mental impairment, severe mental impairment, mental illness and psychopathic disorder.

Moss Side Hospital (Maghull, Liverpool)

This hospital was opened in 1919 for mental defectives. Like Rampton it was transferred to the Ministry of Health in 1947 and was managed by the Board of Control. Like Rampton it takes mentally impaired patients, mentally ill and psychopathic patients. It has an adolescent unit.

Park Lane Hospital (adjacent to Moss Side Hospital)

This hospital opened in 1979 with an advance unit to relieve Broadmoor. It is expanding to accommodate 400 patients of similar classification to those admitted to Broadmoor. As Park Lane increases in size, a long-term rebuilding programme at Broadmoor is going ahead.

Subsequent management of the special hospitals

The four Special Hospitals came under the direct management of the Secretary of State in 1960, when the Mental Health Act 1959 came into operation and abolished the Board of Control.

Eastdale Unit, Balderton Hospital (Nr. Newark, Nottinghamshire)

This Unit, partly supported by central funds, but locally managed, was established in 1974 and provides special rehabilitation facilities for selected patients from the Special Hospitals but mainly from Rampton.

Regional secure units

Following the report of the Butler Committee in 1975, successive

Governments have provided funds for secure unit development in each of the National Health Service Regions. When fully established they will relieve the Special Hospitals of some of their patients, reduce the pressure on prisons and provide some local security for patients who require it. They will probably take some patients remanded for reports or treatment under the new legislation. They will not provide the same degree of security as Special Hospitals and are not intended for long term care. A number of purpose-built units are now in operation, or are about to open and smaller sub-regional or interim units have been taking patients for several years. About 300 beds are available throughout the country in the smaller units. When completed, about 1000 secure beds will be available in the mental health services.

For further details see Bluglass 1978, Royal College of Psychiatrists 1979, the Butler Report 1975 and Gostin 1983.

REFERENCES

Bluglass R 1978 Regional Secure Units and Interim Security for Psychiatric Patients British Medical Journal 1 489–493

Gostin L O (ed) A review of service provisions for mentally ill and handicapped people in England and Wales. Tavistock. London (in press)

Home Office, DHSS 1975 Report of the Committee on Mentally Abnormal Offenders Cmnd 6244 HMSO London (Butler Report)

Royal College of Psychiatrists 1979 Secure facilities for psychiatric patients; a comprehensive policy Royal College of Psychiatrists London

13 Consent to treatment

BACKGROUND

Since 1960, doctors have believed that the Mental Health Act 1959 gave the responsible medical officer the implied authority to treat a detained patient. He was not required to seek the consent of any other person, although good practice indicated that, as far as it was possible, he should obtain the agreement of the patient and consult relatives. If necessary, however, the doctor could override the refusal of a patient who was considered to be irrational and when psychiatric treatment was thought to be in his best interests. This view of the doctor's responsibility and authority was supported by the Department of Health and Social Security although it has never been tested in the courts. Indeed, Sir Keith Joseph, as Secretary of State for Health and Social Security, said in the House of Commons on 23rd January 1973 (Hansard Vol. 849, Column 77) 'I am advised that in the case of a patient detained for treatment under the Mental Health Act, any recognised form of treatment which is considered necessary for such a disorder may lawfully be administered without the consent of the patient. Where, however, the patient is capable of understanding what is proposed, it is the normal practice to explain this to him and, if possible, to obtain his agreement'. Some organisations and writers on the subject have questioned the basis for this interpretation of the law and have suggested that the justification for detaining the patient should be clearly separated from the question of his competence to accept or reject psychiatric treatment.

CONSENT TO MEDICAL TREATMENT

In the field of general medicine a patient may be given treatment for his physical illness only with his real and informed consent. The patient must have explained to him and be capable of understanding precisely what it is that is being proposed and to which he is giving consent. Consent in the absence of reasonable explanation is insufficient (Chatterton v. Gerson and another, 1980, Robertson 1981). The implications of a procedure should be explained, but this does not require an excess of technical detail or the possibility of upsetting the patient by referring to small but inevitable risks. The doctor might reasonably expect that the patient will be likely to accept his advice, just as he accepted the invitation to enter hospital for treatment, but the patient has a fundamental right to determine his own fate, to choose to reject medical advice if he so wishes and to decide to leave hospital even if his decision to do so might mean that he remains in pain, continues to suffer or even that he may be accepting a risk to his life. Treatment given without the consent of the patient is a battery, a form of trespass to the person, which can lead to an action in both the criminal and the civil courts. Failure to provide sufficient information so that consent is not informed might be regarded as negligent.

Although it is commonly assumed that the consent of the nearest relative authorises a physician to treat an unwilling or uncertain adult patient, the relative's consent has no validity in law. The physician will, of course, obtain one or more second opinions from colleagues and will discuss the matter with the relatives when it is necessary to obtain support for a course of treatment proposed for a patient whose capacity to provide informed consent is uncertain, but his eventual decision will depend upon the circumstances of the case, the degree of urgency, the immediate risks to his patient and his ethical duty to act as a doctor within his competence to save life or prevent an immediate deterioration of the patient's condition. His legal authority is derived from the common law.

CONSENT AND INFORMAL PSYCHIATRIC PATIENTS

An informal (voluntary) psychiatric patient is in the same position as an informal physically ill patient. He has the same right to refuse treatment and treatment cannot be administered without the patient's consent except in cases of 'urgent necessity'.

CONSENT AND DETAINED PSYCHIATRIC PATIENTS

The detained patient is in a different situation. His condition has warranted compulsory admission to hospital although it cannot be assumed that he is necessarily always incompetent to understand the nature, purpose and likely effects of a proposed treatment and to give or withhold his consent to its administration. However, some detained patients, because of the nature and severity of their disorder may be unable to give informed consent, or, because of disordered judgment, irrational fears, or other abnormal mental functioning refuse treatment, even though the doctor's explanations are understood. In these cases a specific statutory authority to treat the patient without consent may be required if the patient is to be given the treatment he needs.

AN AUTHORITY TO IMPOSE TREATMENT

The nature of the authority that should be provided in new legislation has been the subject of fierce debate during the past six years. On one side it was argued that decisions about competency are entirely legal matters, outside the province of doctors who prescribe treatment. The medical profession, on the other hand, considered that only doctors are professionally equipped, as a result of their training, to carry out a comprehensive evaluation of the patient's mental state and to make an assessment of his ability to give informed consent. The initial proposals to define a legislative approach which were presented by the Government of the day in 1978 (White Paper 1978) were strongly opposed by the medical profession as over-restrictive and unacceptable, as decisions about consent were to be delegated to a lay panel. The Bill originally laid before Parliament prior to the present legislation made new proposals which required a second independent medical opinion in specified cases. These proposals were more acceptable in principle but again encompassed such a wide range of treatments or diagnostic tests that they were considered likely to constrain psychiatric practice unreasonably. It seemed that almost every investigation carried out, or treatment given, would need a second opinion. It was predicted that about 15 000 second opinions might have been required annually in England and Wales (Beedie & Bluglass 1982), or, in two Birmingham Hospitals studied, approximately seven second opinions would have been required in each hospital weekly.

During the course of the debates in Parliament new proposals were presented by the Government and ultimately accepted with some modifications. They have now been incorporated in the Mental Health Act 1983. It is the first time that *statutory* legislation has been made about treatment consent and is an important step, particularly because its authority extends at one point to include informal (non-detained) patients. This extension applies to treatments of 'special concern' which are subject to the verdict of a multidisciplinary panel before the treatment can be given. The patient must also be able to consent. Although the Act is otherwise almost entirely concerned with detained patients, it was suggested at a late stage in Parliament, during the Report stage of the Mental Health (Amendment) Bill, that if the detained patient required special protection from such treatments being given improperly, then the informal patient should have such protection also. The opposition spokesman, Mr Terry Davis MP requested that *all* patients who might receive treatments 'of special concern' should have the protection of the new procedures. The Government did not oppose the suggestion and it was, therefore, carried. The medical profession expressed its anxiety but little more could be done. With respect to this particular group of treatments, therefore, even though a patient is fully competent and able to provide or withhold informed consent he is obliged to submit to the decisions of an independent group of assessors, who are not all medically qualified, and who will confirm that his consent is indeed valid. This introduces a new principle into the field of medical practice and the law which may, in time, have implications for specialties, other than psychiatry, where at the present time the question of consent to treatment is relatively ill-defined.

BASIC PRINCIPLES

1. The patient's informed consent is required before certain designated treatments can be administered to *patients detained under a section which authorises treatment.*

2. If the patient is unable to give informed consent in relation to these treatments or irrationally refuses consent, treatment may be given only if the opinion of a second independent psychiatrist is in agreement and after he has consulted other non-medical members of the clinical team who know the patient.

3. Some specified treatments 'of special concern' may be given only with the *patient's informed consent*, the endorsement of the validity of that consent by *an independent panel*, together with the clinical approval of an *independent psychiatrist* after he has consulted other members of the clinical team. These opinions are required when the specified treatments are to be given to *detained or informal patients*. For this group the consent of the patient is an absolute requirement.

4. Medication (not included in the arrangements outlined in the previous paragraphs) may be given without the patient's consent and without the need to obtain a second opinion *for up to three months*. After this period of time consent or the endorsement of an independent psychiatrist is necessary to continue. Long-term administration requires a periodic report at the time of renewal of the detention order.

5. A second opinion may be given for a *treatment plan* involving several treatments given over a period of time.

6. The patient may withdraw consent. Continuation of treatment without the consent of the patient would then require the approval of an independent psychiatrist.

7. *Urgent treatment* involving the use of treatments, controlled in other circumstances may be given to patients detained for treatment without consent, or a second opinion for defined purposes.

8. *Urgent treatment for physical illness* (not mentioned in the Act) may be given with the authority of the common law but non-urgent treatment for physical illness would normally require the patient's consent. The criteria facing the doctor are those applicable to an informal psychiatric patient and any patient under medical or surgical care.

9. Any treatment which has not been specified as one which requires any of the procedures described above may be given to a detained patient (for instance, nursing care, occupational therapy, rehabilitation).

10. The Secretary of State, with advice, will list the treatments to be included in each category in Regulations and may change the category from time to time.

11. Independent second medical opinions will be given by psychiatric members of the Mental Health Act Commission or doctors appointed by the Commission to perform this task on behalf of the

Secretary of State (obtained by telephoning the relevant Commission Office; see Appendix).

CONSENT TO PSYCHIATRIC TREATMENT (PART IV)

Application

1. These arrangements and requirements apply to any patient liable to be *detained* under the Act *for treatment*, with the exception of Section 57 which applies to both *detained and non-detained patients*.
2. The consent to treatment requirements *do not apply* to the following:
a. patients detained in an emergency (Section 4) for 72 hours.
b. Informal patients detained for 72 hours under Section 5 to prevent them leaving hospital.
c. Patients detained in a place of safety for 28 days awaiting transfer to hospital (Section 37).
d. Patients removed to a place of safety under Section 135.
e. Patients detained in a place of safety by a police constable (Section 136).
f. Conditionally discharged patients (Sections 42(2), 73 & 74.
g. Patients remanded by a court to hospital for a report to be made (Section 35).
3. The consent to treatment requirements *do apply* to the following:
a. patients detained for assessment and treatment (Section 2).
b. Patients detained for treatment (Section 3).
c. Patients detained on a Hospital Order (Section 37) or an Interim Hospital Order (Section 38).
d. Patients detained on a Hospital Order with restrictions (Section 41).
e. Convicted prisoners transferred to hospital (Section 47).
f. Other prisoners transferred to hospital (Section 48).
g. Patients detained under the provisions of the Criminal Procedure (Insanity) Act 1964 (not guilty by reason of insanity and unfit to plead).
h. Patients remanded for treatment by a Court (Section 36).

TREATMENT REQUIRING CONSENT AND A SECOND OPINION (SECTION 57)

Form of Treatment

a. Any surgical operation for destroying brain tissue or for destroying the function of brain tissue.
b. Such other forms of treatment as may be specified by the Secretary of State in regulations. (Initially, *the surgical implantation of hormones* is to be the only treatment specified).

Conditions

No patient (detained or informal) may be given a treatment in this section (treatment for mental disorder) unless:
a. he has consented to it;
b. an independent doctor and two other persons appointed by the Secretary of State (not being doctors) have certified in writing that the patient is capable of understanding the nature, purpose and likely effects of the proposed treatment and has consented to it; and

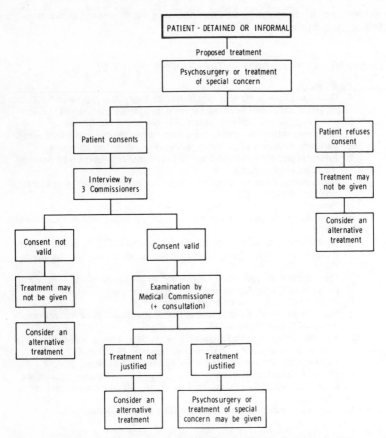

Fig. 13.1 Treatments requiring consent and a second opinion

c. the independent doctor has certified in writing that, having regard to the likelihood of the treatment alleviating or preventing a deterioration of the patient's condition, the treatment should be given.

d. Before giving his clinical opinion the independent doctor is required to consult two other persons who have been professionally concerned with the patient's medical treatment. One of these persons must be a nurse and the other neither a nurse nor a doctor.

TREATMENT REQUIRING CONSENT OR A SECOND OPINION (SECTION 58)

Form of treatment

a. such forms of treatment as may be specified by the Secretary of State in Regulations. (*Electro-convulsive therapy* is, initially, to be the only treatment specified.)

b. The administration of medicine by any means (not included in Section 57) if three months have elapsed since the first occasion

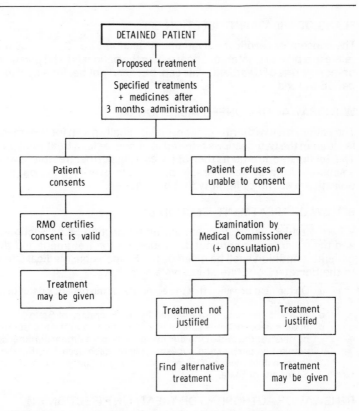

Fig. 13.2 Treatments requiring consent or a second opinion

during his period of detention that the medicine was first administered to the patient . (The Secretary of State may alter this time period by order.)

Conditions
No detained patient may be given a treatment listed as in this Section (forms of medical treatment for mental disorder) unless:

a. He has consented to it and either the Responsible Medical Officer, or an independent doctor, has certified in writing that the patient is capable of understanding the nature of the treatment, its purpose and likely effects and has given consent, or

b. An independent doctor has certified in writing that the patient is *not* capable of understanding the nature, purpose and likely effects of the treatment *or* has not given consent, but that, having regard to the likelihood of its alleviating or preventing deterioration of his condition, the treatment should be given.

c. Before giving his clinical opinion the independent doctor is required to consult two other persons who have been professionally concerned with the patient's medical treatment. One of these should be a nurse and the other neither a nurse nor a doctor.

PLANS OF TREATMENT (SECTION 59)

The consent or certificate given under Section 57 or Section 58 may relate to a plan of treatment under which the patient is to be given one or more forms of treament. This can, but need not be, for a specified period of time.

WITHDRAWAL OF CONSENT (SECTION 60)

The patient may withdraw his consent, if initially given for treatments in either of the two Sections referred to above, or for a treatment plan. The Section requirements then apply as if any further treatment were a separate form of treatment. In practice, to over-rule the patient's objection a scond opinion would be required.

REVIEW OF TREATMENT (SECTION 61)

Where a patient is given treatment under Section 57 or Section 58, and the treatment is continued, a report on the treatment and the patient's condition shall be given by the Responsible Medical Officer to the Secretary of State at intervals as follows:

    a. On the next occasion that the authority for the patient's detention is renewed.
    b. At any other time if so required by the Secretary of State.
    c. In the case of patients subject to a restriction order the report must be given at the end of the first six months (if treatment commenced within this period) and subsequently on each occasion that the Responsible Medical Officer is statutorily required to report to the Secretary of State.

RENEWAL OF AUTHORITY FOR TREATMENT (SECTION 61)

The Secretary of State may request a review of the authority to treat the patient and a further second opinion at any time.

URGENT TREATMENT (SECTION 62)

1. The consent of the patient (detained or not detained) and/or a second independent medical opinion is *not* required as described above for any of those treatments

    a. which is immediately necessary to save the patient's life; or
    b. which (not being an irreversible treatment) is immediately necessary to prevent a serious deterioration of the patient's condition; or
    c. which (not being irreversible or hazardous) is immediately necessary to alleviate serious suffering by the patient; or
    d. which (not being irreversible or hazardous) is immediately necessary and represents the minimum interference necessary to prevent the patient from behaving violently or being a danger to himself or to others.

2. Where the patient has withdrawn consent and a second opinion may be necessary, or, similarly where the Secretary of State has

asked for a second opinion, the Responsible Medical Officer may continue to give treatment already started under a treatment plan if discontinuing the treatment would, in his opinion, cause serious suffering to the patient.

Irreversible treatment: (referred to above) refers to a treatment which has unfavourable, irreversible, physical or psychological consequences.

Hazardous treatment: (referred to above) refers to a treatment which entails significant physical hazard.

Doctors must decide whether or not a treatment is hazardous or irreversible.

TREATMENT NOT REQUIRING CONSENT (SECTION 63)

The consent of a patient is not required for any medical treatment given to him (for mental disorder) if it is not treatment requiring the procedures (consent and/or a second opinion) laid down in Sections 57 and 58, but the treatment must be given by or under the direction of a Responsible Medical Officer.

Comment: Although consent and/or a second opinion is not required, it remains good practice to seek the patient's consent and co-operation in so far as it is possible. In some cases a second opinion might be indicated. The treatments defined by statute are treatments for which consent and/or a second opinion are *a mandatory legal requirement*. Treatments given in any other circumstances remain subject to the general application of the prevailing standards of good medical practice and ethics.

PRACTICAL IMPLICATIONS

The application of the new legislation to *informal* patients, or even out-patients, day-patients or the patients of family doctors or neurologists is fairly clear. Any treatment maybe prescribed and the ordinary law and ethics apply, as discussed earlier in this chapter, with the exception of psycho-surgery and any other treatments that the Secretary of State specifies in Regulations is subject to Section 57 (that the consent of the patient and a second opinion are both necessary). In the three-year period 1979–1982, psycho-surgical operations were performed on 207 informal patients and four detained patients in England and Wales. (Official Report of the Special Standing Committee 1982.) This Section will, therefore, be of most concern to the relatively few psychiatrists and neurosurgical centres with a special interest in stereotactic brain surgery for the relief of some intractable forms of mental illness.

At the time of writing it has been decided to include only one other form of treatment in this section; the surgical implantation of hormones to reduce male sexual drive. Other treatments could be added in the future, but only after very careful consideration.

Apart from the treatments discussed above, which equally concern detained patients and informal patients, any treatment can be given to a *detained* patient (detained for treatment) from the outset, even though he may object or be unable to consent, if the doctor considers that it is necessary, unless it is specified in Regulations as a treatment for which the patient's consent is required, or a second opinion, should it be indicated. One form of treatment, electroconvulsive therapy (ECT), will be in this category (Section 58) requiring consent or a second opinion from the outset. Other treatments may be specified in time. Any medicine not specified as requiring consent and/or a second opinion from the outset may be given for up to three months. At the end of this period of time many patients will have recovered or even been discharged from the detention order. Many, who would have been unable to consent competently at an earlier stage will now be capable of doing so, and consent, but no second opinion will be required to continue the treatment because the patient will be competent to consent. Some others will, however, require a second opinion from an independent medical commissioner (or doctor appointed for the purpose). A further estimate of the possible need for a second opinion, carried out in a study of two hospitals in Birmingham suggested that with the final legislation on consent, about one second opinion would be required weekly in an average mental hospital (Beedie & Bluglass 1983).

THE PATIENT'S CONSENT

It should be noted that the Responsible Medical Officer has the responsibility of confirming that the patient has consented to the proposed treatment and certifying that he is competent under the requirements of Section 58 of the Act. The patient's consent must be informed. The Act requires, specifically, that he is capable of understanding the nature, purpose and likely effects of the proposed treatment and has then given his consent, but it is the Responsible Medical Officer who must certify that he is capable of this degree of understanding. However, Parliament did not consider that it could require the Responsible Medical Officer to certify that although capable of understanding, the patient *did actually understand* the nature, purpose and likely effects of the treatment, but the patient's consent, if he is competent, would presumably imply that he did so understand if it is to be informed consent.

It is important, therefore, that the Responsible Medical Officer personally explains the treatment to the patient and does not delegate this task to a nurse, junior doctor or some other person. He should give his explanation clearly, simply and patiently, in words that the patient can reasonably be expected to understand, avoiding technical jargon, but without going into too much detail or listing uncommon side-effects which might unreasonably upset the patient. The right balance is difficult to define, although some reference has been made to it in judgments involving the treatment of physically ill patients (Robertson 1981). The explanation should be as complete and comprehensive as possible and sufficient to allow a competent patient to give a valid and informed consent. The extent to which details may be withheld on the grounds that a nervous patient may be seriously upset by them is a matter of judgment, but if there is doubt it would be good practice to obtain a second opinion, even if one was not clearly required by law.

The ability to communicate in both directions is obviously important. The patient should be able to understand the doctor and the doctor should be able to understand the patient. Cultural or language difficulties, speech defects or deafness, must be overcome in appropriate ways – by the use of interpreters, communicating by writing or any other helpful but valid aid. Again, if there is any doubt about the level of understanding, a second opinion must be obtained.

ASSESSING COMPETENCY

The patient must be *capable* of understanding:

    a. the *nature* of the proposed treatment. The Responsible Medical Officer should explain simply what procedure the patient will experience and what will be done to him; that he will receive a periodic intramuscular injection or the procedures involved in having ECT, for instance.

    b. The *purpose* of the proposed treatment – not simply that it will make him better; but it is expected that his depression will begin to lift over a period of time, or that his sleep pattern will improve in time and quality, or that appetite will improve, for instance. Time should be taken to discuss these matters in some detail and for the patient to ask questions.

    c. The *likely effects* of the treatment, this includes not only the expected benefits, but also the most likely side-effects, if any, and what will be done to try and avoid or diminish them. The patient ought to be presented with alternative strategies to be followed if the outcome is less successful than is hoped.

If the patient cannot follow all this because of the nature and influence of his mental disorder, or if there is any doubt, then the Responsible Medical Officer should request a second opinion. If the patient is clearly capable of understanding but withholds consent, yet the Responsible Medical Officer is convinced that the treatment would be of substantial benefit to the patient, then he should ask for a second opinion.

In some cases the patient will appear to understand the nature, purpose and likely effects, but may not agree that he is ill. It is unlikely that his consent can be regarded as real and informed consent. Others may understand, but either consent to, or refuse treatment under command of a hallucinatory voice or the influence of paranoid delusions about the treatment. In all these instances the validity of the patient's consent is in doubt and an independent second opinion should be obtained.

A patient's reasonable questions should be answered. If a patient asks, for instance, about the risk of any specific side-effects, and if he is rational and competent he has a right to know the answers; unless the information would be against his best interests and would unduly disturb and distress him.

It should be remembered that the requirements under the Act are designed not only to protect the patient but also to protect the doctor and his colleagues. If the procedures are carefully followed then there is a sound basis for a defence against any formal criticism or any legal action.

CONSULTING THE CLINICAL TEAM

Although the Responsible Medical Officer must make the final decision he should discuss the treatment options with other members of the clinical team who know the patient. This usually means the nursing staff, social worker, occupational therapist and sometimes the psychologist (but psychologists are not necessarily involved with every patient on the ward). As far as it is possible, it is valuable to have the agreement of the experienced members of the team to a particular course of treatment, but the Responsible Medical Officer is the team leader, is able to weigh up all the factors and must take the final responsibility. In most cases the team will work together and be in agreement. If a second opinion is required then the independent doctor is required to *consult* a nurse and one other person (neither a nurse nor a doctor). This is likely to be a social worker or occupational therapist, unless a psychologist knows the patient well, when he may be the staff member consulted. The independent doctor is not limited to consulting two professional members of the team; that is a minimal requirement. If the case has been well discussed beforehand a conflict of opinion between members of the clinical team will be unlikely. If conflict exists, the second doctor will have to make a final and independent judgment. The decision is *his* to make after consultation.

'THE TREATMENT SHOULD NOT BE GIVEN'

In some cases the independent appointed doctor providing a second opinion will decide that the treatment should not be given. It is suggested that in these circumstances every effort should be made to assist the Responsible Medical Officer to find an alternative approach to treatment, which might, of course, involve another treatment requiring the second doctor's approval. It may be assumed that both doctors are concerned to help the patient and Responsible Medical Officers should always be prepared to accept that on occasions a treatment proposed will not be supported. It is likely that this will not be a frequent experience.

However, the Act does not prevent the Responsible Medical Officer requesting another appointed doctor to give an opinion, although the Commission may provide guidelines on the provision of a third (or more) opinions.

URGENT TREATMENT AND SHORT-TERM PATIENTS

The Section on *urgent treatment* applies with reference to treatments otherwise controlled by Section 57 and Section 58. It relieves the doctor of the necessity of obtaining the patient's consent and/or a second opinion for those treatments if it is necessary to give them to patients (detained for treatment) in an urgent situation. This Section does *not* apply to patients on *short-term sections* of seventy-two hours duration since they are primarily detained for *assessment* and Section 57 and Section 58 do not apply to them. This does not mean that in an emergency the doctor may not treat a disturbed patient to relieve him, in his best interests, but the legal authority to do so is derived from the common law rather than from Section 62 (urgent treatment). The doctor in a case of urgency might be expected to decide appropriately to treat the patient but there is no real authority *in the Mental Health Act* to do so; the legal protection is a common law protection.

PATIENTS IN PRISONS

Prison Medical Officers are not infrequently presented with serious dilemmas when attempting to treat a mentally disturbed prisoner while awaiting the outcome of efforts to find a bed for him in a National Health Service Hospital. Since the prisoner is not detained under the Mental Health Act for treatment there is no authority to treat the patient without his consent. Every co-operative effort must, therefore, be made to transfer to hospital patients requiring treatment which can only be given with the authority of the Act.

Guidance
It is expected that the Mental Health Act Commission will offer advice and guidance concerning the operation of this Part of the Act and may include specific guide-lines in the Code of Practice.

MENTAL HEALTH ACT COMMISSION: CONSENT TO TREATMENT

The Commission has appointed ninety doctors to provide second opinions for Sections 57 and 58 in addition to the 23 Medical Commissioners. They are contacted through the Regional Commission Office (see Appendix) which nominates the doctor who

will visit to see the patient. The appointed doctor is requested to
attend within forty-eight hours to consider ECT and within one
working week with respect to medicines. The Responsible Medical
Officer must decide whether or not a form of treatment is one which
is encompassed by the provisions of Section 57 and 58. He is also
responsible for ensuring that a nurse and another person
professionally concerned with the patient's treatment is available for
consultation. Two names must appear on the certificate authorising
treatment in the absence of consent for the form to be valid. The
Commission has also emphasised that generally the doctor in
charge of the treatment should present a 'plan of treatment' for
consideration by the appointed doctor which might indicate the
approach to the patient's treatment during the next weeks or
months. This should include mention of the number of treatments
proposed (for ECT) and the duration of the anticipated course of
treatment. For medicines, the category of treatment as classified in
the British National Formulary may be used rather than specific
preparations within the category which remain a matter of clinical
judgment.

The Commission will be issuing further guidance to doctors about
the arrangements for reviewing at intervals treatment given with the
authority of a second doctor (Section 61). The RMO is required to
report to the Commission on each occasion that detention is
renewed, with respect to a patient being treated on the authority of
an appointed doctor. Similar arrangements will be made with
reference to restricted patients.

REFERENCES

Beedie M A, Bluglass R 1982 Consent to Psychiatric Treatment: Practical
    Implications of the Mental Health (Amendment) Bill British Medical Journal
    284 1613–1616
Beedie M A, Bluglass R 1983 Mental Health Act (Letter). British Medical
    Journal 287 360
Chatterton v Gerson and another 1981 All ER 257 The Times London 7th
    February 1980 p. 25, col 1 British Medical Journal 1980 Medico-legal Report
    p 574
DHSS, Home Office, Welsh Office, Lord Chancellor's Department 1978 A
    Review of the Mental Health Act 1959 Cmnd 7320 HMSO London
House of Commons 1982 Official Report of the Special Standing Committee on
    the Mental Health (Amendment) Bill Part II 29th June 1982 p 832 HMSO
    London
Lawton, Lord Justice 1983 Legal aspects of iatrogenic disorders: discussion
    paper. Journal of the Royal Society of Medicine 76 289–291
Robertson G 1981 Informed Consent to Medical Treatment The Law Quarterly
    Review January 102–126

14 Mental Health Review Tribunals

BACKGROUND

Mental Health Review Tribunals, although constituted by the Mental Health Act, are independent bodies whose members are appointed by the Lord Chancellor. They provide the opportunity for patients to have their detention reviewed and give a right of appeal should they object to being kept in hospital or under guardianship compulsorily.

CONSTITUTION AND POWERS OF MENTAL HEALTH REVIEW TRIBUNALS

There is a Mental Health Review Tribunal for each of the fourteen National Health Service Regions for England and there is one Tribunal for Wales.

The Lord Chancellor must appoint legal, medical and lay members to Tribunals.

Lay members are appointed after consultation with the Secretary of State for Social Services and must have such knowledge of social services or other qualifications as the Lord Chancellor considers suitable.

Medical members are appointed after consultation with the Secretary of State for Social Services and are usually senior consultant psychiatrists. The medical member is required to examine the patient privately and make any clinical enquiries necessary. He may examine medical records to form an opinion of the patient's clinical state. He will often need to visit the hospital for this purpose before the Tribunal sits.

Legal members are appointed by the Lord Chancellor and they must have such legal experience as he considers necessary. The legal member is the President of the Tribunal. The new Act provides that legal members who preside at hearings concerning restricted hospital order patients must be designated for this purpose by the Lord Chancellor (and will probably be circuit judges or lawyers of at least equivalent rank and experience).

Each area has a Tribunal Chairman, a lawyer, who appoints as members of Tribunal panels at least one legal member, one medical member and one lay member. The legal member must act as

President, but if the Chairman serves on a Tribunal he must preside.

The Lord Chancellor is responsible for the rules of procedure for Tribunal hearings. They were drawn up last in 1960 (with some subsequent amendments) and are being reviewed at the present time.

Hearings, which normally take place at the hospital, can be formal or informal and can be public. There are rules governing each kind of hearing. An *informal hearing* allows everyone interested in the application to come before the Tribunal at the same time unless, for special reasons, the Tribunal decides to exclude anyone. The applicant, the responsible authority and any person notified are entitled to appear and take part if the Tribunal considers it proper. Witnesses may be called.

A public hearing can only be considered where a formal hearing has been allowed. Patients detained in hospital or under guardianship have a right to apply to a Tribunal to have their case reviewed at intervals. The nearest relative has a periodic right to request that the patient's case is referred to a Tribunal for review. The Secretary of State for Social Services (and the Home Secretary in relation to restricted patients) may refer a patient's case to a Tribunal at any time. All these rights of application or referral are extended by the new legislation. It is expected that consequently there will be many more Tribunal sittings in the future with an increase from 904 sittings in 1980 to approximately 5000 sittings a year.

Previously the Tribunal's powers were limited to discharging the patient or the reclassification of the category of mental disorder justifying detention. The Mental Health Review Tribunal had no authority over a restricted patient; it could only advise the Home Secretary who had no obligation to accept the advice.

PRINCIPAL CHANGES

1. As indicated earlier, the period before the detention of a patient (detained for treatment) must be renewed has been halved. Previously the patient could apply to a Tribunal once in the first 12 months, once in the second 12 months and so on. Now he has the opportunity to apply once in the first six months, once in the second six months and then annually. He, therefore, has twice as many opportunities to apply to a Tribunal.

2. Patients detained for assessment (for 28 days) also have the right to apply to a Tribunal, not previously available to them.

3. Restricted offender patients have a new right to apply at intervals directly to a Tribunal (not simply requesting the Home Secretary to refer the case).

4. There are new arrangements for the automatic review of a patient's case. The managers of the hospital are required to refer a non-offender patient to a Tribunal for review after the *first six months* if the patient has not exercised his right to apply, himself. The

managers must also refer the case of any detained patient who has not exercised his right to make an application during the *next three years*. The arrangements for automatic reviews became operative during the Autumn of 1982.

5. Tribunals have a new authority to discharge restricted patients (not simply to advise the Home Secretary) and for all patients they have a wider range of options when deciding a case.

6. Previously legal aid was available to assist applicants to Tribunals to prepare a case. Now a further limited form of assistance has been authorised by the Lord Chancellor: legal assistance by way of representation (ABWOR). This means that the patient may be provided with a lawyer to represent him and the costs of medical and legal expert advice will be met.

RIGHTS OF APPLICATION TO A MENTAL HEALTH REVIEW TRIBUNAL

PATIENTS DETAINED UNDER PART II OF THE ACT (Section 66)

The Mental Health Act 1983 provides a right of application to a Mental Health Review Tribunal to a patient or nearest relative in the following categories:

1. A *patient* detained for assessment (Section 2) may apply *within 14 days* of admission to hospital.
2. A *patient* detained for treatment (Section 3) may apply *within six months* of admission to hopsital.
3. A *patient* who is received into guardianship (Section 7) may apply *within six months* of the date of the order.
4. A *patient* or *nearest relative* may apply *within 28 days* of the date they were informed of the patient's Mental Health Act diagnostic reclassification (Section 16).
5. A *patient* who is transferred from guardianship to hospital (Section 19) may apply within *six months* of the date of transfer.
6. A *patient* who is detained in hospital for treatment or who is subject to guardianship may apply to a Tribunal within each period following renewal of the order (first six months following renewal, then during each subsequent 12-month period) (Section 20).
7. *The nearest relative* of a patient detained for treatment who has requested the discharge of the patient may apply *within 28 days* of being told that a report of the Responsible Medical Officer prevents the discharge (Section 25).
8. When a *nearest relative* of a patient detained in hospital or subject to a guardianship order has had his authority removed by a County Court order, he may apply to a Tribunal *once every 12 months* (Section 29).

PATIENTS DETAINED UNDER PART III OF THE ACT

Unrestricted patients

A right of application to a Mental Health Review Tribunal is provided for the following offender patients to whom no restrictions on discharge apply, or to their nearest relative.

1. A *patient* or *nearest relative* may apply *within 28 days* of being notified of a diagnostic reclassification under the Mental Health Act.
2. A *patient* who is transferred from a guardianship order to a hospital order may apply *within six months* of the date of transfer.
3. A *patient* subject to a transfer direction from prison, or a guardianship order may apply *within the first six months* of the order being made and then within each subsequent period of renewal.
4. A *patient or nearest relative* of a patient subject to a hospital order may apply in the *second six months* of the patient's detention and in any subsequent period of 12 months (Section 69).
5. A *patient* who is subject to any other transfer direction or who is subject to a guardianship order may make an application *within six months* of the direction or order being made.
6. The *nearest relative* of a patient who is subject to a guardianship order may apply *within 12 months* of the order being made and *once a year.*

POWERS AND PROCEDURES OF TRIBUNALS

APPLICATIONS TO TRIBUNALS

Background

Applications from patients or relatives maybe made by writing to the office of the appropriate Mental Health Review Tribunal for the area. (Addresses are listed in Appendix of this book.)

One application may be made within each authorised period. For example, for patients detained for treatment (Section 3) *one* application only may be made in the first six months, *another* in the second six months of detention and so on.

Principal change

The 1983 Act makes clear that an application that has been made, but withdrawn in accordance with Tribunal rules, must be disregarded and should not prevent another application to the Tribunal being made. Revised procedural rules are likely to require the agreement of the Chairman of the Tribunal before an application is withdrawn to ensure that the withdrawal is not the result of improper influence or has not been decided on without consideration.

POWERS OF TRIBUNALS

Background

After considering an application, a Tribunal *may* direct that a detained patient is discharged. In certain circumstances the patient *must* be discharged. The function of the Tribunal is primarily to decide whether it continues to be appropriate to detain the patient, not whether treatment is or is not required.

Principal changes
1. Since the grounds for the initial detention for assessment or for other reasons have been substantially revised in the new legislation, the grounds for determining when the patient must be discharged have changed in parallel. They differ for patients who were admitted for assessment.

2. The Act requires the Tribunal to consider certain matters when deciding whether or not to discharge a patient.

3. The Tribunal is now given more flexibility when discharging a patient. Instead of being restricted to discharging or not discharging, alternative options are now provided.

4. New powers are given to the Lord Chancellor when formulating Tribunal rules.

TRIBUNAL DISCHARGE OF UNRESTRICTED PATIENTS (Section 72)

The Tribunal has the discretionary power to discharge any detained patient. The circumstances in which a patient *must* be discharged are described below.

PATIENTS DETAINED FOR ASSESSMENT

Purpose
Mental Health Review Tribunal consideration of the need to continue to detain a patient for assessment (and necessary treatment).

Grounds
A Tribunal *shall direct* the discharge of a patient liable to be detained under Section 2 of the Act if they are satisfied:
i. that he is not then suffering from mental disorder, or from mental disorder of a nature or degree which warrants his detention in a hospital for assessment (or for assessment followed by medical treatment) for at least a limited period, or;
ii. that his detention is not justified in the interests of his own health or safety or for the protection of others.

PATIENTS DETAINED UNDER OTHER SECTIONS (EXCLUDING RESTRICTED PATIENTS)

Purpose
Mental Health Review Tribunal consideration of the need to detain a non-restricted patient for reasons other than for assessment.

Grounds
A Tribunal *shall direct* the discharge of a patient liable to be detained otherwise than under Section 2 of the Act, if they are satisfied:
i. that he is not then suffering from mental illness, psychopathic disorder, mental impairment or severe mental impairment; or
ii. although suffering from one of these forms of mental disorder it is not of a nature or degree which makes it appropriate for him to be liable to be detained in hospital for medical treatment (the disorder is not of sufficient severity); or

iii. that it is not necessary for the health or safety of the patient, or for the protection of other persons, that he should receive such treatment.

iv. Where the managers refuse a nearest relative's request to discharge the patient because, in the Responsible Medical Officer's opinion, it would be dangerous to do so, the relative may apply to the Tribunal. If the Tribunal does not consider that the patient would be likely to behave in a dangerous manner if released, then they must discharge him.

DETERMINING FACTORS IN OTHER CASES

In determining whether or not to direct the discharge of a patient (other than a patient detained for assessment) whose case is not included in the grounds i) to iv) above (when the patient *must* be discharged) the Tribunal is required to consider:

a. the likelihood of medical treatment alleviating or preventing a deterioration of the patient's condition; and

b. in the case of a patient suffering from mental illness or severe mental impairment, to the likelihood of the patient (if discharged) being able to care for himself; to obtain the care he needs or to guard himself against serious exploitation.

These requirements do not restrict the discretion of the Tribunal to decide whether or not to discharge a patient but they are, in effect, guidance about the matters that the Tribunal should bear in mind.

DELAYED DISCHARGE

It is often important to give time for arrangements to be made for the patient's accommodation, care or supervision in the community before discharging him. Previously the Tribunal would formally delay a decision for this purpose but it was considered preferable to empower the Tribunal to direct the patient's discharge on a future date.

A Tribunal, under this Section may alternatively:

a. recommend that the patient be granted leave of absence;
b. be transferred to another hospital;
c. be transferred into guardianship.

The Tribunal may give further consideration to the case if any of these recommendations are not implemented.

PATIENTS SUBJECT TO GUARDIANSHIP

BACKGROUND

The Tribunal has a similar discretionary power to discharge any patient who is subject to guardianship. The Tribunal *must* discharge a patient when the grounds for continuing the order are not met.

PRINCIPAL CHANGES

1. The wording of this section is revised to take account of the new definitions of 'mental disorder'.

2. Instead of considering whether continuation of guardianship would be 'in the interests' of the patient (as previously), the Tribunal must now consider whether it would be 'in the interests of the welfare of the patient'.

Purpose
Mental Health Review Tribunal consideration of the need to continue a guardianship order.

Grounds
A Tribunal *shall* direct the discharge of a patient who is subject to a guardianship order if they are satisfied:
a. that he is not suffering from mental illness, psychopathic disorder, mental impairment or severe mental impairment; or
b. that it is 'not necessary in the interests of the welfare of the patient', or for the protection of other persons, that the patient shall remain under guardianship.

RECLASSIFICATION

When a Tribunal decides not to discharge a patient from an order, it may change the form of mental disorder on the application, order or direction detaining the patient. It may, for instance, conclude that the patient is suffering from mental impairment, rather than psychopathic disorder. However, if it does so, the grounds for detaining a patient with the new form of mental disorder must be fulfilled.

AUTOMATIC REFERRALS TO A MENTAL HEALTH REVIEW TRIBUNAL

Previously many patients did not take the opportunity to make an application to a Mental Health Review Tribunal to have their detention reviewed. They may have lacked the ability or the initiative to make an application or they may not have been aware of their rights to do so. Similarly the nearest relative may not have been aware of his right to refer the case. Often, of course, the patient and relative accept the need for detention or guardianship and they are aware that there are no grounds for taking up the Tribunal's time and challenging the medical and nursing staff. If the relationships between patient and relative, and his doctor and the nurses caring for him is a good one, then there is frequently no ground for disagreement which may impair treatment.

The new provisions are regarded as a safeguard for patients and staff to ensure that the patient's detention is continued for no longer than is absolutely necessary. It provides the opportunity for a periodic independent review of the need for continued detention where a patient has not exercised his right to apply to a Tribunal himself, or his relative has not referred the case.

GENERAL PRINCIPLES

1. The hospital managers must refer to a Mental Health Review Tribunal the case of any patient detained for treatment, or subject to an unrestricted hospital order, who has not had a Tribunal hearing in the first six months of detention. This requirement presupposes that the patient has had the authority for detention renewed for a second six months.

2. The hospital managers are also required to refer patients detained for treatment, or subject to an unrestricted hospital order, if three years (one year if the patient is under 16 years of age) have elapsed since his case was last considered by a Tribunal.

3. The previous two requirements ensure that a patient who is under the age of 16 has his case reviewed after the first six months of detention and then at annual intervals.

4. The patient has a right to be examined independently by a doctor of his own choice to provide a report on behalf of the patient in connection with an automatic referral by the managers.

5. The time periods at which the managers must refer a case to a Tribunal, as above, may be altered by order of the Secretary of State and after approval by a resolution of each House of Parliament. This might arise if the time periods are found with experience to be too long or too short.

6. If an application to a Tribunal, although made, was withdrawn, the managers must disregard it.

7. These requirements apply to patients detained in mental nursing homes in the same way as for patients detained in hospitals.

8. Automatic references of long-stay patients to Tribunals commenced in October 1982, using powers existing under Section 57 of the 1959 Act.

INITIAL AUTOMATIC REFERRAL

Purpose
Duty of the managers of hospitals to refer cases to a Mental Health Review Tribunal.

Grounds
The managers of a hospital *must* refer the following cases to a Tribunal:
a. a patient admitted to hospital for treatment (Section 3) who has not exercised his right to apply to a Tribunal and for whom no application or reference has been made under any section of the Act.
b. A patient who is transferred from guardianship to hospital but does not exercise his right to apply to a Tribunal and for whom no application or reference has been made under any Section of the Act.

Requirement
The managers *must* refer the case to a Tribunal at the expiration of the period for making an application (six months).

LONGER-TERM AUTOMATIC REFERRAL

Purpose
Duty of the managers of a hospital to refer a long-stay case to a Mental Health Review Tribunal.

Grounds
The managers *must* refer the following to a Tribunal: a patient detained under the Act who has had his detention renewed.

Requirement
The managers *must* refer the case to a Tribunal at the expiration of a period of three years since his case was last considered by a Tribunal (or, if the patient is under 16, at the expiration of a period of one year).

INDEPENDENT EXAMINATION

Any doctor authorised by, or on behalf of a patient, may at any reasonable time visit and examine the patient in private. He may require the production of records relating to the detention or treatment of the patient in hospital and he is authorised to inspect them.

PATIENTS OF UNDER 16 YEARS OF AGE

Patients who are under 16 years of age have the same rights of application to a Tribunal as do adults. Previously there were restrictions on the right of a young patient to apply to a Tribunal.

TRIBUNAL RULES OF PROCEDURE

The Mental Health Act 1983 authorises the Lord Chancellor to make rules of procedure relating to the making of applications to Tribunals, the proceedings and related matters.

Particular points for which provision must be made in Rules are listed in the Act, but the Lord Chancellor may make any other necessary rules.

PRINCIPAL CHANGE

1. An additional requirement allows for the Lord Chancellor to provide by Rule for the Chairman of aTribunal to settle preliminary and incidental matters on his own. This allows some matters to be clarified or dealt with before the Tribunal of three people meet.

2. A new provision gives those attending a Tribunal as applicant, patient, witness or representative (other than lawyers) a clear entitlement to expenses.

3. Another member of the Tribunal may be nominated to act in the Chairman's absence.

GENERAL POWER TO MAKE PROCEDURAL RULES

The following summarises specific matters in relation to which the Lord Chancellor may make particular provision:

a. to enable a Tribunal (or its Chairman) to postpone an application for a period of time specified in the Rules (but for not more than 12 months).
b. For the transfer of proceedings from one Tribunal to another, if for instance, the patient moves to another area.
c. For restricting the persons qualified to serve as members of a Tribunal for the consideration of an application.
    This may apply to a specific class of application.
d. For enabling a Tribunal to deal with an application without a formal hearing, where the applicant has not requested it and it would be detrimental to the patient's health.
e. For enabling a Tribunal to exclude members of the public, or any particular group, from the proceedings. The Tribunal may also, by Rules, prohibit the publication of reports of proceedings or mention of the names of anyone concerned in the proceedings.
f. For regulating the circumstances and the person who may represent applicants and patients.
g. For regulating the methods by which relevant information may be obtained and given to the Tribunal. Rules may also authorise Tribunal members to visit and have a private interview with the patient.
h. For making relevant documents or details or oral information available to an applicant or patient unless it is not in the interests of the patient or for other special reasons.
i. For requiring a Tribunal, if so requested, in accordance with the Rules to provide statements of the reasons for any decision, unless it would not be in his interest to provide such a statement to a patient.
j. For conferring on Tribunals such ancillary powers as the Lord Chancellor thinks necessary to carry out his functions.
k. For enabling any functions of a Tribunal which relate to matters preliminary, or incidental, to an application to be performed by the Chairman of a Tribunal.

ASSISTANCE BY WAY OF REPRESENTATION (ABWOR)

During the course of the debates on the new legislation it was evident that a strong lobby was exerting pressure on the Government to make available some form of legal aid and assistance to patients wishing to put a case to a Tribunal. This also received wide support from Peers and Members of Parliament of all parties.

Consequently the Lord Chancellor announced his intention to extend the Legal Aid Scheme to include *legal representation* for all applicants to a Tribunal from 1st December 1982 under the Assistance by Way of Representation (ABWOR) Scheme. The DHSS gave details of the scheme in November 1982 (Circular HN (83) 37).

Up to this point legal assistance under the Green Form Scheme was available to help patients and other applicants of limited means to prepare their cases. This covers all work carried out by a lawyer short of instituting proceedings. Such Advice and Assistance did not, however, cover legal representation at MHRT hearings (although some solicitors did appear without payment). The 'Green Form Scheme' continues, but now representation is also available. It extends the Green Form Scheme to assistance given by a lawyer to an applicant in instituting and conducting proceedings, including the representation of the patient. Only the applicant may receive the assistance (*either* the patient or the nearest relative or other person), but where the case has been referred to the Tribunal by the Minister, the patient is treated as the applicant and may claim ABWOR.

Procedure

The patient must undergo a simple assessment of his resources, carried out by a solicitor, to ensure that he qualifies on financial grounds. Then, if he does qualify he may receive assistance under the Green Form Scheme. Where ABWOR is sought, the patient must obtain the approval of the Law Society.

The Green Forms are available from the Law Society Legal Aid Centres. A List of Legal Aid Centres in England and Wales is in the Appendix.

Hospital managers and any member of staff including social workers may obtain advice from the centres to assist those detained patients who have no access to solicitors or legal advice.

TRIBUNALS FOR RESTRICTED PATIENTS

Rules under Section 78 of the Act allow the person who may act as President of a Tribunal hearing the case of a restricted patient to be limited to persons of certain qualification (a Circuit Judge or equivalent).

NEW CODE OF PROCEDURAL RULES

In June 1983 the Lord Chancellor signed a new code of procedural rules to which the reader is referred. The rules expand the general powers (above). The distinction between formal and informal readings is removed. The rules do not prescribe the use of specific forms.

15 Discharge of restricted patients

BACKGROUND

Previously, under the 1959 Act, a patient detained as a consequence of a Hospital Order, but subject also to a restriction order, could not apply directly to a Mental Health Review Tribunal to have his case reviewed. The patient's case could be referred to a Tribunal at any time by the Home Secretary for advice, and after 12 months detention the patient could request the Home Secretary to do so, but neither the patient nor his nearest relative could apply directly. Further, the Tribunal could not direct the discharge of the patient, but only advise the Home Secretary. The Home Secretary in his turn would take into account the opinion of the Aarvold Committee (see Chapter 11).

The changes now made in the law result from the decision of the European Court of Human Rights in the case of X v the United Kingdom in 1981 which was briefly referred to in Chapter 11. The European Convention on Human Rights which came into force on the 3rd September 1953 gave specific legal content to human rights in an international agreement, and combined this with machinery for supervision and enforcement. The United Kingdom is one of the signatories accepting the right of an individual to petition the European Commission and the jurisdiction of the European Court of Human Rights which sits in Strasbourg.

The case of X v the United Kingdom concerned a conditionally discharged Broadmoor patient who was subsequently recalled. He wished to challenge the grounds for his recall and he included among his subsequent complaints to the European Court, his objection that in England there was no procedure which would allow the lawfulness of his detention in hospital to be reviewed speedily by a court. The European Court ruled that the United Kingdom was indeed in breach of the European Convention on Human Rights and that although Mr X was lawfully detained, conditionally discharged patients who are recalled should be told speedily of the reason for recalling them and a restricted patient should be entitled to a periodic review of his case by a court. The patient should be released if his continued detention was not justified because he no longer suffered from mental disorder. It was not justified to detain a person *in a hospital* for any reason other than for the treatment of his mental disorder.

The Government was, therefore, under an obligation to make new arrangements which are now included in the 1983 Act.

Definitions
A 'restricted patient' means a patient who is subject to a restriction order (from a court) or a restriction direction (e.g. for a prisoner transferred to hospital).

RIGHT OF RESTRICTED PATIENTS TO APPLY TO A MENTAL HEALTH REVIEW TRIBUNAL
Review Tribunal
A restricted patient detained in hospital may apply to a Tribunal

 a. in the period between the expiration of six months and the expiration of 12 months beginning with the date of the relevant hospital order or transfer direction; and

 b. in any subsequent period of 12 months.

Reference by Secretary of State
1. The Secretary of State (Home Secretary) *may* refer the case of a restricted patient to a Tribunal at any time.

 2. The Home Secretary *must* refer the case of a restricted patient who has not been considered by a Tribunal within the last three years.

 3. The Home Secretary may by order vary the period referred to in the previous paragraph.

 4. The reference of a conditionally discharged patient must be made to the Tribunal for the area in which the patient resides.

Discharge of patients
There are separate criteria to be considered by Tribunals when considering the discharge of *restricted patients* which differ from the criteria to be considered in relation to *non-restricted patients* (discussed on p. 93).

Absolute discharge
1. A Tribunal *must* direct the absolute discharge of a restricted patient if it is satisfied:

 a. that he is not now suffering from mental illness, psychopathic disorder, mental impairment or severe mental impairment, or from any of those forms of disorder of a nature or degree which makes it appropriate for him to be detained in hospital for medical treatment (i.e. he may suffer from a mild form of disorder not justifying detention) or

 b. that it is not necessary for the health or safety of the patient or for the protection of others that he should receive such treatment, and

 c. that the Tribunal are satisfied that it is *not* appropriate for the patient to be liable to recall (i.e. to be *conditionally discharged*).

2. Where a patient is absolutely discharged the hospital order and restriction order cease to have effect.

Conditional discharge
1. If it is appropriate for the patient to remain liable to recall the patient may be *conditionally discharged*. Only a restricted patient may be conditionally discharged.

   a. He may be recalled at any time by the Home Secretary.
   b. The patient must comply with any conditions imposed by a Tribunal at the time of his discharge or imposed at any subsequent time by the Home Secretary. The Home Secretary may alter the conditions, whether imposed by him or the Tribunal, at any time.

2. Where a restriction order is removed *after* a patient has been conditionally discharged the patient shall cease to be liable to be detained.

Deferred conditional discharge
A Tribunal may defer the decision to discharge a patient conditionally until suitable arrangements have been made (for accommodation and supervision, for example). This gives time for the hospital to make arrangements for him. If the patient makes a further application to a Tribunal during a period of deferment the second Tribunal takes over responsibility for any further decisions regarding the patient.

Powers of the Home Secretary
Although Tribunals may make decisions as described above, the Home Secretary retains his powers to discharge a patient himself, terminate restrictions at his discretion and to consult the Aarvold Committee.

TRIBUNAL DECISIONS FOR PATIENTS SUBJECT TO RESTRICTION DIRECTIONS

1. Following their consideration of a patient who is subject to a restriction direction, the Tribunal

   a. must notify the Home Secretary if they consider the patient would be entitled to be absolutely or conditionally discharged if he were on a hospital order made by a court with restrictions on discharge. (A patient subject to a restriction direction may be liable to return to *prison* in such circumstances.)
   b. If the Tribunal notifies the Home Secretary that the patient would be entitled to be conditionally discharged, they may recommend that if it is decided not to discharge him he should continue to be detained in hospital.

2. If the Tribunal does *not* recommend that a patient entitled to be absolutely or conditionally discharged should continue to be detained in hospital if not discharged, then, if the patient had originally been transferred from prison, the Home Secretary may

direct that he is returned there (or to whichever institution he came from).

3. If the Tribunal recommended absolute or conditional discharge for a patient subject to a restriction direction, the recommendation becomes operative if the Home Secretary notifies the Tribunal that it must discharge the patient within a period of *90 days* beginning with the date that the Tribunal notified the Home Secretary of their decision.

4. If the Home Secretary does not notify the Tribunal that the patient may be discharged as recommended by the Tribunal within 90 days, then the managers of the hospital must return the patient to prison (or other originating institution).

5. When a patient is returned to prison his liability to be detained in hospital ceases to have effect.

6. The Home Secretary may return a patient to prison at his own discretion, if he is still liable to be returned, without the involvement of a Tribunal.

PATIENTS RECALLED TO HOSPITAL

1. When a conditionally discharged patient is subsequently recalled to hospital, the Home Secretary must refer his case to a Mental Health Review Tribunal *within one month* of the patient's return.

2. The patient's rights of application to a Tribunal recommence as if a new restriction order or restriction direction had commenced on the date of his recall.

3. A restricted patient who has been conditionally discharged but not recalled to hospital may apply to a Mental Health Review Tribunal

   a. in the period between the expiration of 12 months and the expiration of two years beginning with the date on which he was conditionally discharged; and
   b. in any subsequent period of two years. Any application should be made to the Tribunal for the area in which the patient resides.

4. If a patient does apply as with the preceding paragraph the Tribunal may

   a. vary any condition which may impose or add a condition
   b. remove the restrictions absolutely.

PROCEDURE AND COMPOSITION OF TRIBUNALS

The power of the Secretary of State to make rules relating to the Tribunal's proceedings are extended with respect to restricted cases as follows:

   a. The Secretary may make provision for the restriction of persons qualified to serve as President of a Tribunal considering a restricted patient. The Rules will probably stipulate that the President in these circumstances will be a lawyer of the rank of Circuit Judge (or equivalent) thus forming a link between the Crown Court, which may impose restrictions and the Tribunals which may remove them.

b. The Secretary of State may make provision for the transfer of the consideration of a case from one Tribunal to another, where appropriate (for instance, where a patient moves to reside in an area served by another Tribunal).

PERSONS TREATED AS RESTRICTED PATIENTS

1. The arrangements for restricted patients apply to the following groups of patients transferred to hospital with a restriction direction*

   a. A person who is detained during Her Majesty's Pleasure.
   b. Those found unfit to plead or not guilty by reason of insanity (under the Criminal Procedure (Insanity) Act 1964).
   c. Those who, on appeal against conviction, are found by the Court of Appeal to be either unfit to plead or not guilty by reason of insanity.
   d. Those in respect of whom the Court of Appeal substitutes a finding of unfitness to plead for a former verdict of not guilty by reason of insanity.
   e. Patients transferred with restrictions into the English mental health system from Northern Ireland, the Channel Islands or the Isle of Man, or from Scotland.

2. The Secretary of State is required to refer to a Tribunal the case of a patient treated as subject to a hospital order with restrictions transferred under the Criminal Procedure (Insanity) Act 1964 at the expiration of the first six months of detention, if the patient has not previously made an application himself. The Court would have been obliged to order the person to hospital (if unfit to plead or not guilty by reason of insanity) but it is not required to consider grounds for continued detention in hospital. The patient is, therefore, given a right of early consideration of these matters by a Tribunal.

3. No account should be taken of any applications to a Tribunal made by a patient but withdrawn.

*NOTE: Persons treated as restricted patients in 1. a–e above and Section 47 and Section 48 transferees have an additional right of application to a Tribunal in the *first six months* of their detention which is not available to patients on a Hospital Order (with or without restrictions).

16 The removal and return of patients within the United Kingdom (Part VI)

(and other related matters)

BACKGROUND

The Mental Health Act's powers generally apply only to England and Wales. Other parts of the United Kingdom have separate mental health legislation.

Northern Ireland patients are subject to the Mental Health Act (Northern Ireland) 1961, the Isle of Man and the Channel Islands have their own jurisdictions, and the Scots have the Mental Health (Scotland) Act 1960; although at the present time a Bill is proceeding through Parliament to amend the Scottish Act and new mental health legislation is likely to become operative there in the near future.

It is occasionally necessary for a patient to be transferred from England to another part of the United Kingdom. It may be possible to discharge the patient, when he can be admitted to a hospital elsewhere, either informally or compulsorily as necessary. Other patients, who are detained in hospital in England or are under guardianship, may require a continued power to detain them during a journey, on a train or boat, and while awaiting admission to another hospital. The Act makes the necessary provisions for the conveyance and transfer of the various categories of patient to ensure that a patient can be transferred without a break in the authority for his detention.

The 1959 Act was subsequently subject to amendment to take account of the 1960 Scottish Act and the 1961 Northern Ireland Act. The provisions for the transfer of patients within the United Kingdom have not been subject to amendment by the Mental Health (Amendment) Act and are, therefore, reproduced in the Mental Health Act 1983. However, the new Scottish Mental Health Act will inevitably contain amendments to change the Mental Health Act 1983 to incorporate the updated Scottish legislation to the extent that the English Act must make reference to the Scottish one. The provisions for the removal of alien patients have been revised (see p. 108).

REMOVAL OF PATIENTS TO AND FROM SCOTLAND

Non-restricted patients

1. A patient liable to be detained without restriction on discharge (except patients remanded for report or treatment, or subject to an interim hospital order) or a patient subject to guardianship, may be removed to Scotland if it is in his interests, and directions may be given by the Secretary of State for taking him there, if arrangements have been made for the patient's reception to a hospital or registered mental nursing home (or for receiving him into guardianship).

2. If the patient was liable to be detained in hospital immediately before removal (or was subject to guardianship) he will be treated on reception in Scotland for all purposes as if he were subject to the equivalent section of the Scottish Mental Health Act.

3. Where a patient, was, immediately before transfer to Scotland subject to an order admitting him to hospital for assessment, he will be treated in Scotland as if he had been admitted subject to an emergency recommendation under the Scottish Act, made on the date of admission.

4. If the patient was subject in England to a transfer direction (he had been a convicted prisoner for instance) he shall be treated as if the sentence had been imposed by a court in Scotland.

Restricted patients

1. Where patients are subject to an order restricting discharge of limited duration, the expiry date of the restriction order does not change on transfer.

2. Restriction orders of unlimited duration remain subject to the Secretary of State. In England the Home Secretary is responsible; in Scotland the Secretary of State for Scotland has the responsibility for 'Secretary of State patients'. A patient who returns to England during the period that a restriction order is in force remains liable to the Home Secretary's jurisdiction (powers to grant leave or to recall the patient) while the restriction order remains in force.

Removal of patients from Scotland to England

Reciprocal arrangements as above apply to patients liable to be detained under the Scottish Act if they are removed to England. The Secretary of State has powers to make appropriate orders.

Removal of patients to and from Northern Ireland

Similar arrangements as above provide for the movement of patients between England and Northern Ireland.

REMOVAL OF OTHER PATIENTS TO AND FROM ENGLAND AND WALES

To and from the Channel Islands and Isle of Man

Background
The 1959 Act made provisions for the transfer of certain patients *from* the Channel Islands or the Isle of Man to England and Wales. The patients concerned are offenders who have been detained in hospital under island legislation but require hospital facilities which are only available in England or Wales. Powers also exist to return such patients to their home islands at the appropriate time. The above powers continue in the new Act.

Principal changes
1. The 1983 Act makes further provision to allow the removal to the Channel Islands or to the Isle of Man of patients detained in hospital in England or Wales or subject to guardianship. This allows patients to be moved so that they are near their friends, relatives or homes and also takes account of the problems of visitors from the islands who become ill while on the mainland.

   2. The grounds for removing a patient to the Channel Islands or to the Isle of Man are defined:

Removal of patients from the Channel Islands or Isle of Man
1. The Secretary of State (Home Secretary) is empowered to direct, by issuing a warrant, that an offender found by a court in the Channel Islands or the Isle of Man to be insane, to have been insane at the time of an alleged offence, or to be not guilty by reason of insanity, to be removed to a hospital in England or Wales.

   2. Such a patient shall, on his reception in England or Wales, be treated as if he had been removed to hospital following a similar finding in a court in England, that is to say, as if on a hospital order with restrictions on discharge.

   3. Any patient moved to a hospital in England or Wales from Islands as above may be returned to the Island from which he was removed to be dealt with as he would have been, had he not been removed.

Removal of patients to the Islands
1. The Secretary of State may authorise that a patient liable to be detained in hospital in England or Wales or subject to guardianship, is removed to the Channel Islands or the Isle of Man, and may give necessary directions for conveying him there.

   2. It must appear to the Secretary of State (Home Secretary) that it is in the interests of the patient and that arrangements have been made to admit him to a hospital or to receive him into guardianship. This is a similar provision to the arrangements for transferring a patient to Scotland or Northern Ireland.

Removal of non-offender patients from the Channel Islands or the Isle of Man.

1. New provision is made in the 1983 Act to remove non-offender patients to a hospital in England or Wales if the patient is subject to provisions in the Islands corresponding to detention or guardianship power in England.

2. The patient must be detained in England or Wales on arrival as though detained under the corresponding order or application in the 1983 Act. He is subject then to the same safeguards as other patients including the corresponding rights of appeal to a Mental Health Review Tribunal.

3. Patients who were transferred from prison to hospital in the Islands are treated as if sentenced in England. (The length of the prison sentence is taken into account when removing restrictions.)

4. Restriction orders or directions continue in England as they would have done in the Islands.

REMOVAL OF ALIEN PATIENT FROM ENGLAND, WALES OR NORTHERN IRELAND

Background

It is occasionally considered necessary to move a mentally ill alien patient to his country of origin. An alien patient is a person of another country of origin who does not have a right of abode in the United Kingdom. The 1959 Act gave the Secretary of State wide powers which included the power to move informal patients, patients subject to guardianship and those on short-term sections. The provisions have now been drastically restricted. It was considered illiberal that, for instance, an informal patient detained under Section 5 (detention of an informal patient receiving treatment in hospital) could be liable to compulsory removal out of the country.

Only about seven alien patients have been removed anually in recent years.

General principles

1. The categories of patient for whom authorisation for removal may be given are limited to patients detained under the longer-term sections of the Mental Health Act 1983 and the Mental Health Act (Northern Ireland) 1961. (Legislation provides that matters affecting aliens cannot be dealt with under Northern Ireland statutes.)

2. No patient may be removed without the approval of a Mental Health Review Tribunal. This ensures that an independent body reviews the circumstances every time it is proposed to remove an alien from England or Wales.

3. In the case of restricted patients who are removed, powers of recall continue to apply while a restriction order is in operation, should the patient return to England or Wales. Similarly should a patient liable to be detained, return, he remains liable to be detained.

Removal of alien patients

1. The power to remove alien patients applies only to patients:

    a. detained in hospital for treatment under the Mental Health Act 1983 or similarly under Section 12 of the Mental Health Act (Northern Ireland) 1961;

    b. detained on a hospital order under Section 37 of the Mental Health Act 1983, or similarly under Section 48 of the Mental Health Act (Norther Ireland) 1961; or

    c. subject to an order or direction under either of the Acts which have a similar effect to a hospital order.

2. The Secretary of State shall only exercise his powers with the approval of a Mental Health Review Tribunal, or in the case of a patient in Northern Ireland, the Mental Health Review Tribunal for Northern Ireland.

3. Where a restriction order is in force it shall continue to apply to the patient if he returns to England or Wales at any time before the end of the period for which the order would have continued in force.

17 Management of property and affairs of patients

BACKGROUND

As already indicated in the discussion on the historical origins of mental health legislation, the early legal references to the mentally disordered were concerned with property. The *Statute de Praerogativa Regis* which probably dates from the time of Edward II, claimed a royal prerogative to the wardship of lunatics and idiots and of their property: this power and duty of the monarch was recognised even earlier and was subsequently delegated to the Lord Chancellor and then to other judges, thus laying the foundations of the Court of Protection.

A general duty is placed upon local social service authorities to protect any 'moveable property' of a client who is admitted as a patient to a hospital (National Assistance Act 1948, Section 48 (1)). The Act defines the circumstances in which action should be taken and the authority to carry it out (for instance to enter premises and to take charge of items of property).

Some patients, whether detained in hospital or not, are so ill as a result of physical or mental disorder that they are incapable of managing their own affairs and the purpose of the Court of Protection is to take this responsibility for them.

The Mental Health Act authorises the continuity of the Court of Protection as part of the Supreme Court (not the High Court) for the protection and management of the property of persons 'under disability'. The Court is staffed by judges nominated by the Lord Chancellor from the members of the Chancery Division of the High Court who are experienced in dealing with matters concerning property. In addition to 'nominated judges' the Lord Chancellor appoints a Master of the Court of Protection and other 'nominated officers'.

The court has jurisdiction where, after considering medical evidence, the judge is satisfied that a person is incapable, by reason of mental disorder, of managing and administering his property and affairs. Such a person is 'a patient' in this context and there is no assumption (as there was under the old lunacy laws) that compulsory detention automatically infers incompetence in taking decisions about these matters. In fact, incapable patients might not be in hospital but may, for instance, be in the care of a relative.

The court is authorised to take action in an emergency where a judge has reason to believe, on evidence, that a person *may* be incapable of manging his property or affairs, by reason of mental disorder.

GENERAL FUNCTIONS OF THE COURT OF PROTECTION

1. The judge has the general function to 'do or secure the doing of all such things as appear necessary and expedient':

    a. for the maintenance or other benefit of the patient;
    b. for the maintenance or other benefit of members of the patient's family;
    c. for making provision for other persons or purposes to whom, or which, the patient might be expected to provide if he were not mentally disordered; or
    ·d. otherwise for administering the patient's affairs.

2. The court's principal concern is for the patient, and it has a wide discretionary power to take decisions to meet the patient's debts and other obligations. It must have regard for the interests of creditors who may not be able legally to enforce their claims because of the patient's mental disability.

3. The court has control over all the property and affairs of a patient under its jurisdiction and it must be consulted when any decision has to be taken or anything is needed for the patient in relation to his property or finances.

The court may, on the patient's behalf, make orders or give directions for a wide range of matters which are specified in the Act, although this list is not exclusive. It includes:

    a. the control and management of the patient's property;
    b. the buying or selling of property;
    c. carrying on the patient's profession, trade or business by appointing a suitable person to do so;
    d. dissolving a partnership of which the patient is a member;
    e. carrying out the patient's contracts;
    f. conducting legal proceedings (including divorce proceedings) on his behalf;
    g. reimbursing people, such as relatives, who have looked after and maintained the patient;
    h. exercising any legal power vested in the patient;
    i. making a will on his behalf;
    j. exercising his powers as a patron (Lord Chancellor only).

4. The court has special powers concerning the appointment of trustees and has the power to appoint a receiver (usually a member of the patient's family) to carry out the court's directions. Authority is given to the court relating to the vesting of any stock (such as shares, a fund, annuity or other similar asset) which stands in the name of a

mentally disordered person, in a curator appointed outside England or Wales. A further section deals with the preservation of interests in a patient's property so that it may be maintained during the period of the patient's incapacity. This is but a limited summary of the court's powers and for detail the reader is referred to the legal authorities.

APPLICATIONS TO THE COURT OF PROTECTION

1. Anyone may make an application to the Court of Protection. If the patient has little property a relative, friend, social worker or official may make direct application to the Chief Clerk, Court of Protection, Staffordshire House, 25 Store Street, London WC1E 7BP, or to the Personal Applications Branch at that address. If the patient's estate is large, the applicant would be best advised to instruct a solicitor to act for him.

2. The court will send forms which will require a written statement to be sworn before a Commissioner for Oaths (an affidavit) containing medical evidence of the patient's incapacity which should be provided by the doctor responsible for the patient's treatment (not necessarily a doctor approved under the Mental Health Act). A further affidavit will give particulars of the patient's background and circumstances.

3. The patient should be given notice that an application has been made and he has to the hearing date, or seven clear days (whichever is later), to write to the court. He has a right to object, preferably with medical evidence, if he maintains that he is not incapable of managing his affairs.

The court may not inform the patient if it considers that he would be incapable of understanding the notification, or it would be injurious to his health. As far as possible, the court will try and accommodate the patient's wishes, if it is in his interest.

In any case of doubt about the patient's mental state, a Medical Visitor will be requested to examine the patient and report to the court (see below).

LORD CHANCELLOR'S VISITORS

The Act authorises the Lord Chancellor to appoint Medical, Legal and General Visitors of patients known as Lord Chancellor's Visitors. A *Medical Visitor* is a doctor with special knowledge and experience of mental disorder. *Legal Visitors* must be barristers or solicitors of not less than ten years standing. *General Visitors* are not required to possess either a legal or medical qualification for appointment (no qualifications are, in fact, specified).

It is the duty of the Visitors to visit patients at the direction of the judge to investigate the capacity of a patient to manage and administer his property and affairs. The Visitor may interview and examine the patient in private and a Medical Visitor may carry out a medical examination and may require the production of medical records for inspection. His report is confidential.

There are two full-time Medical Visitors appointed at the present time to assist the Court of Protection, but the Lord Chancellor has decided to transfer most of their responsibilities to General Visitors, officers of the court. Due to the burden of their work the Medical Visitors in recent years have only visited, on a routine basis, patients who are being cared for in their own homes or in nursing homes and often on only one occasion. The Consultant in charge has reported upon hospital patients. Under the 1983 legislation a General Visitor is normally required to visit, unless the judge specifically requests, because of the circumstances of the case that the visit should be made by a Medical or Legal Visitor.

In 1983 some 23 000 persons were under the jurisdiction of the Court of Protection.

The above is necessarily only a summarised account of the law relating to the Court of Protection. For more details the reader is referred to the list of references and to the 1983 Act itself.

FURTHER READING

Gostin L O 1983 The court of protection. London. MIND.
Heywood N A & Massey A 1971 Court of Protection Practice 9th Ed. by Hunt D G, Reed M E & Whiteman R A London. Sweet & Maxwell.
Hoggett B 1976 Mental Health London Sweet & Maxwell.

18 Approved Social Workers (Mental Welfare Officers)

BACKGROUND

The Mental Health Act 1959 provided for Mental Welfare Officers to replace the 'duly authorised officer' under previous legislation for the purpose of carrying out various functions under the Act. Principally he has had the duty of making applications for the admission of patients to hospital or to guardianship if he is satisfied that an application should be made and the relative does not wish to do so himself (or no relative can be found).

Originally Mental Welfare Officers were social workers with a special expertise and knowledge of psychiatric problems and they worked harmoniously with their medical colleagues. During the past decade and the introduction of the 'general purpose' social worker based on a social service department, this expertise was lost and the social workers acting as Mental Welfare Officers often had limited experience of the issues involved. This caused increasing concern, discussed in the White Paper of 1978. It was concluded in that document that an improvement in standards and training was necessary. The recommendations were adopted for the purposes of the Mental Health Act 1983.

PRINCIPAL CHANGES

1. The Mental Health (Amendment) Act provided for the functions under the Mental Health Act 1983, at present carried out by Mental Welfare Officers, to be transferred to 'Approved Social Workers' starting two years from the passing of the Mental Health (Amendment) Act. Approved Social Workers will therefore, commence their duties on the 28th October 1984. This will give time for training to be given and for appointments to be made.

2. The Act imposes a *duty* on local social service authorities to appoint a *sufficient number* of Approved Social Workers for the purpose of discharging their functions under the Act.

3. No person may be appointed as an Approved Social Worker unless he is approved by the authority as having appropriate competence in dealing with persons who are suffering from mental

disorder. In giving approval the authority is required to have regard for 'such matters as the Secretary of State shall direct'.

It is intended that social workers will as a result be 'approved' in a similar way to the approval of doctors for the purposes of the Act. The Department of Health has consulted appropriate bodies to agree the form of training and method of approval which the Secretary of State will require local authorities to adopt. It issued guidance early in 1983 to ensure that training programmes may be established. A local authority would not, however, be prevented from appointing a suitably experienced person as an Approved Social Worker if he clearly had appropriate competence to carry out the functions required under the Act.

Powers of entry and inspection

Section 115 of the Act provides that an Approved Social Worker may, at all reasonable times produce (if asked to do so) some duly authenticated document showing that he is a social worker and may enter and inspect any premises (that are not hospital premises) if he has reason to believe that a mentally disordered patient is not under proper care. This authority applies to premises within the area of the local authority in which such a patient is living.

REFERENCE

DHSS, Home Office, Welsh Office, Lord Chancellor's Department 1978 Review of the Mental Health Act 1959 Cmnd 7320 HMSO London.
Central Council for Education and Training in Social Work 1983 Regulations for the Assessment of Approved Social Workers. CCETSW London.

19 After-care for detained patients

BACKGROUND

Both health and social services authorities have a duty to provide after-care for detained patients when they leave hospital. They should be provided with appropriate social worker support, accommodation such as lodgings, hostels or group homes, according to their needs and appropriate opportunities for rehabilitation in the community. Supervision is usually provided for restricted patients who are conditionally discharged. Paragraph 2(1) of Schedule 8 of the National Health Service Act 1977 provides that a local social services authority *may* make after-care arrangements for those suffering from mental disorder, and to such extent as the Secretary of State may direct *shall* make such arrangements. A Circular, No. 19 of 1974, was issued by the Department of Health requiring local authorities to provide after-care which states that local authorities must provide:

i. residential accommodation for mentally disordered persons;
ii. facilities for training and occupation, including training centres and day centres;
iii. social work support and other domiciliary care and services.

Section 28 of the National Health Service Act 1977 lays a duty on local social service authorities to provide social work support for the health services. Regulations made under the 1977 Act (S.I. 1982/287) similarly require health authorities to provide after-care, which may be given by hospital-based social workers or their colleagues.

Despite these arrangements, which have existed for some time, when the Amendment Bill was debated in the House of Lords there was substantial support for a proposal from Baroness Masham of Ilton to underline and endorse the local authorities' duty to provide after-care by including a requirement to do so in the Mental Health Act. There was similar enthusiasm in the House of Commons. Parliament believed that the authorities had so far often failed to provide the after-care that they were required to make available and they should be given a specific duty to do so by the Mental Health Act.

DUTY TO PROVIDE AFTER-CARE

1. Section 117 provides that under the Mental Health Act 1983 after-care should be provided for patients detained under Section 3 or Section 37 (and Sections 47 or 48) who cease to be detained and leave hospital (but there is no requirement under this Act for after-care to be provided for those detained under the short-term powers).

2. A duty is imposed on the District Health Authority and the local social services authority to provide after-care for patients in these categories.

Arrangements are to be made in co-operation with relevant voluntary agencies.

3. The after-care must be provided until the District Health Authority and the local social services authority are satisfied that the person concerned is no longer in need of such services.

4. The 'District Health Authority' and 'local social services authority' concerned are those for the area in which the person is resident or to which he is sent on discharge.

20 Code of practice and regulations

BACKGROUND

The Act authorises the Secretary of State to make *Regulations* in general terms for the practical operation of the procedures required by the Act, together with Orders or Rules. It specifies throughout the Act a variety of matters for which provision must be made; for example, prescribing necessary forms, keeping records and making returns, and for ensuring that the functions to be performed by bodies (such as local authorities) or individuals, such as relatives, are carried out.

Regulations are *legally binding* and must be accepted. They will include categories of treatment for which the consent of the patient and/or a second independent opinion is required under the consent to treatment requirements. The Secretary of State is advised by the Mental Health Act Commission in determining which treatments should be listed in regulations and must also consult other relevant bodies.

The Act also provides for a *Code of Practice* which also lists treatments which give cause for special concern or which may do so in certain circumstances. Unlike regulations, the Code of Practice is not legally binding except in relation to treatments of special concern (Section 118(2)) but doctors are expected to take account of it when making decisions about treating a patient and it represents 'good practice'. The Code supplements the provisions relating to consent to treatment and it is prepared by the Mental Health Act Commission on behalf of the Secretary of State who has direct responsibility for it under the Act.

CODE OF PRACTICE

1. Section 118 requires the Secretary of State to prepare, and from time to time, to revise, a Code of Practice.

   a. For the guidance of medical practitioners, managers and staff of hospitals and mental nursing homes and approved social workers in relation to the admission of patients to hospitals and mental nursing homes under the Act.
   b. For the guidance of medical practitioners and members of other professions in relation to the medical treatment of patients suffering from mental disorder.

2. The Code specifies forms of medical treatment, in addition to the treatments listed in Regulations, which give rise to special concern and should not be given unless the patient has consented and certificates have been provided by an independent doctor and others, as required by Section 57.

3. Before preparing the Code or making any alteration to it the Secretary of State is required to consult such bodies as appear to him to be concerned.

4. The Secretary of State is required to lay copies of the Code and of any alterations to it, before Parliament. If either House of Parliament passes a resolution requiring the Code (or any alteration to it) to be withdrawn the Secretary of State must do so and prepare an alternative Code.

5. No resolution may be passed by either House of Parliament in respect of a Code, or alteration to it, after the expiration of a period of 40 days beginning with the day that it was laid before the House. No account should be taken of any period for which the House was adjourned for more than four days.

6. The Secretary of State is required to publish the Code currently in force and will probably direct the Commission to prepare it on his behalf.

Comment

The Act provides that the Code *shall* list treatments of 'special concern' in addition to any specified by Regulations, but it is intended that it will also give guidance on the procedures to be followed in deciding when a patient's consent is valid or when a second opinion should be obtained. It will advise the independent doctor on the principles to be followed when deciding whether or not a form of treatment should be given and when a second opinion should be considered. It is likely that the Code will also refer to treatments for forms of illness other than mental disorder, from which the patient may be suffering. It may also refer to the principles to be kept in mind when treating patients in an emergency.

It is intended that guidance on good practice relating to all aspects of the care and treatment of patients formulated by the Commission will also be included in the Code which will be updated from time to time, as decisions are made and advice is given. The multidisciplinary membership of the Commission allows contributions to the discussions leading to the formulation of advice, to come from a representative group with wide and developing knowledge of all the issues concerned. Doctors providing second opinions are often members of the Commission and this also assists the Commission in gaining experience.

Although the Code of Practice does not (with one exception) have the force of law, courts and professional bodies dealing with civil actions or complaints against doctors are likely to take account of evidence of failure to observe the advice and recommendations that it provides.

21 The Mental Health Act Commission

BACKGROUND

The first step towards the establishment of an independent body to supervise standards of care for psychiatric patients was taken with the appointment in 1774 of Commissioners in Lunacy with the responsibility of licensing and inspecting private madhouses in London. It consisted of five physicians elected annually by the Royal College of Physicians. They were replaced in 1828 by a body of Metropolitan Commissioners, consisting of 15 members appointed by the Home Secretary, of whom only five were physicians and most of the rest were Members of Parliament. Their powers included (in London) the supervision of hospitals for the insane, in addition to private madhouses (but with the exception of Bethlem). For a short period from 1842 their jurisdiction included provincial hospitals.

The Lunatics Act of 1845 replaced the Metropolitan Commissioners by Lunacy Commissioners appointed by the Lord Chancellor with a permanent full-time inspectorate and central secretariat. In addition to the powers of inspection held by the Metropolitan Commissioners they were given the right to visit the insane in whatever institution they were confined and the Lord Chancellor could order special visits (including a visit to Bethlem). The Lunacy Commission was reconstituted as the Board of Control in 1913 with a continuing responsibility to inspect and supervise standards in all hospitals for the mentally disordered, including the present Special Hospitals, and to scrutinise documents relating to compulsory admission. The Board had the authority to order the discharge of a patient on medical evidence.

The Mental Health Act 1959 abolished the Board of Control and the appeal functions were vested in Mental Health Review Tribunals. As all hospitals were now under the management of the Minister of Health the need for an independent inspectorate was considered unnecessary, but the Royal Medico-Psychological Association (now the Royal College of Psychiatrists) regretted the disbanding of the Board and has never considered that the increasing number of alternative inspectorates with limited powers replaced its wide and authorative function.

The College, with some other organisations, continued to recommend the case for a permanent, independent commission, to protect the interests of the individual psychiatric patient and to promote high standards of care (Bluglass 1981).

The previous Government declared itself unenthusiastic about this proposal and in the White Paper of 1978 considered that there was little support for it, and that it would be wrong in principle to reintroduce a system for psychiatric patients which is fundamentally different from that provided for other patients. It was proposed to introduce an experimental scheme of 'patients' advisers' as an alternative way of safeguarding the position and rights of vulnerable patients, but the 1981 Government took a different view (White Paper 1981). Patients detained under the compulsory powers of the Mental Health Act are in a unique position because they have no right to discharge themselves, unlike all other patients (incuding other psychiatric patients).

It is, therefore, essential that the procedures leading to detention and the renewal of the authority for their detention are subject to scrutiny from a body which is independent of those who have been concerned with the compulsory admission and detention.

The Government accordingly decided to set up a Mental Health Act Commission with a general protective function for detained patients and it accepted the Royal College's view that it should have important responsibilities with reference to the consent to treatment regulations. The establishment of the Commission is the most important innovation in the Mental Health Act 1983 and is likely to exert a very important influence on the development of psychiatric practice in future years.

The Commission has a multidisciplinary membership and has four principal functions:

1. To provide independent medical opinions on consent to treatment.
2. To keep under review the powers of detention under the Act.
3. To prepare, on behalf of the Secretary of State, a Code of Practice.
4. To visit and interview patients detained in hospitals and nursing homes and to investigate individual complaints.

The Commission may also be required to extend its responsibilities to include informal patients.

GENERAL PRINCIPLES

1. The Act empowers the Secretary of State (for Social Services and for Wales together) to establish a 'special health authority' under Section 11 of the National Health Service Act 1977. This Act allows a special health authority to be established at the Secretary of State's discretion for the purpose of performing any functions 'which he may direct the body to perform on his behalf'. A special health authority operates independently but is subject to the directions of the

Secretary of State. The National Health Service Act 1977 provides for the constitution and administration of such a body and the Mental Health Act 1983 directs that this special health authority is called the Mental Health Act Commission.

2. The Chairman and members have been appointed by the Secretary of State who has consulted widely, particularly the professional organisations in selecting suitable experienced and representative people, although the members serve as individuals, not as representatives of any professional group.

3. The Commission consists of a Chairman and, approximately, 12 lawyers, 12 nurses, 12 psychologists, 12 social workers, 12 laymen and 22 psychiatrists – since the medical members have extra duties (giving second opinions and carrying out clinical examinations). The members are chosen for their experience and knowledge of the special problems with which the Commission is concerned and they are likely to be asked to serve for up to four years.

4. The Commission has a central policy committee based in London consisting of members of the Commission who also serve with their other colleagues on one of three regional panels, which have representatives from each membership group.

5. The three regional panels are based at Nottingham, London and at Liverpool. Each panel is responsible for several National Health Service Regions (see Appendix).

Functions and powers of the Commission
The Secretary of State is empowered to direct the Commission to perform three principal functions on his behalf:

1. To appoint medical practitioners on behalf of the Secretary of State, to provide independent second opinions in connection with the consent to treatment requirements.
2. To carry out the functions of the Secretary of State when reviewing the treatment of long-term detained patients.
3. To visit and interview in private, patients who are detained in hospitals and mental nursing homes. It is likely that the Commission will be required to visit at least once a year, but Special Hospitals will be visited once a month.
4. The Secretary of State may 'at the request of, or after consulting the Commission (and any other concerned bodies) direct the Commission' to keep informal patients under review. There was much pressure for this from the professional bodies but it was decided to limit the Commission's remit to detained patients initially. The same rights are given when examining informal patients as for detained patients, to examine the patient in private and to request and examine treatment records.

The Commission is required by the Act to publish a report on its activities in the second year after its establishment and every two years from then onward. The report must be sent to the Secretary of State who will lay a copy before each House of Parliament.

General Protection of Detained Patients

1. The Secretary of State is provided with a responsibility to oversee the use of powers and the discharge of duties imposed by the Act in relation to detained patients, but he must direct the Commission to perform these functions on his behalf. He must make arrangements for his representatives to visit hospitals and mental nursing homes and interview detained patients in private. They are also required to investigate:

    i. any complaint made by a detained patient which the patient considers has not been satisfactorily dealt with by the managers of the hospital; and

    ii. any other complaint as to the exercise of the powers or the discharge of the duties conferred or imposed in respect of a detained patient.

2. The arrangements allow discretion to exclude matters from investigation in circumstances which will be specified or matters which it would be inappropriate to investigate.

3. Members of Parliament may make a complaint to the Commission (on behalf of a patient for instance) and they must receive a report.

Authorised visitors to mental nursing homes

Anyone authorised to visit hospitals to review patients and conditions on behalf of the Secretary of State may at any reasonable time

    1. visit and interview in private any patient in a mental nursing home;

    2. request the production of records relating to detention and treatment and he may inspect them.

    3. A doctor may examine any patient in private.

NOTE: The Secretary of State has appointed Lord Colville of Culross to be Chairman of the Commission from 30th September 1983. A Code of Practice will probably be completed by 1985.

REFERENCES

DHSS, Welsh Office, Home Office, Lord Chancellor's Office 1978 Review of the Mental Health Act 1959. Cmnd 7320 HMSO London

Bluglass R 1981 Towards a new Mental Health Act: Mental Health Commission for England and Wales. Bulletin of the Royal College of Psychiatrists. 130–132 June

DHSS, Home Office, Welsh Office, Lord Chancellor's Office 1981 Reform of Mental Health Legislation Cmnd 8405 HMSO London

REGULATIONS

Mental Health (Hospital, Guardianship and Consent to Treatment) Regulations 1983.

Mental Health Act Commission Regulations 1983.

22 Offences under the act and legal protection of staff

BACKGROUND

The Mental Health Act is a statement of the law in relation to mentally disordered patients. Forms and documents must be completed in accordance with the requirements of the Act and any statements made must be true. Any person who wilfully infringes these requirements is liable to be convicted of an offence under the Act.

It is, in addition, an offence to ill-treat or wilfully neglect patients or for a man to have sexual intercourse with a woman who is severely mentally handicapped. It is an offence for a man who is a member of staff of a hospital to have intercourse with a woman patient in the hospital, or for a male guardian to have intercourse with a woman who is subject to his guardianship. (The Sexual Offences Acts encompass the above *sexual offences*).

It is an offence to assist a person to be absent without leave or to escape from custody or to harbour and assist such a patient.

It is an offence to obstruct an authorised person from inspecting premises, from interviewing or examining a patient or from inspecting documents.

These requirements have been carried over to the 1983 Act from the previous legislation without alteration or are included in other Acts of Parliament. It is not an offence for a woman staff member to have sexual intercourse with a male patient.

Forgery and making false statements (Section 126)

1. It is an offence for a person, with intent to deceive, to forge any of the following:

   a. any application to detain a patient in hospital or admit a patient to guardianship;

   b. any medical recommendation or report under the Act;

   c. any other document required or authorised to be made for any of the purposes of the Act.

2. It is an offence for a person, with intent to deceive to use a forged document or to allow another person to use it. It is an offence to make or have in his possession any document which he knows to be

forged or a document which resembles a genuine one but is intended to deceive.

3. Any person who wilfully makes a false entry or statement in any application, recommendation, report, record or other document under the Act with intent to deceive is guilty of an offence. So is any person who makes use of any such entry, or statement with intent to deceive.

4. A person found guilty of an offence as above is liable

    a. on summary conviction, to imprisonment for a term not exceeding six months or to a fine not exceeding the statutory maximum; or to both or

    b. on conviction on indictment, to imprisonment for a term not exceeding two years, or to a fine of any amount, or both.

5. 'Forge' has the meaning given in the Forgery and Counterfeiting Act 1981.

Ill-treatment of patients (Section 127)

1. It is an offence for any person being an officer on the staff of, employed in, or one of the Managers of a hospital or mental nursing home:

    a. to ill-treat or wilfully neglect a patient who is receiving treatment for mental disorder as an in-patient in that hospital or home; or

    b. to ill-treat or wilfully neglect on the premises of which the hospital or home forms part, an out-patient.

2. It is an offence for any individual to ill-treat or wilfully neglect a mentally disordered patient who is subject to guardianship or who is otherwise in that individual's custody or care (whether by virtue of any legal or moral obligation or otherwise).

3. Any person guilty of an offence under this Section is liable:

    a. on summary conviction, to imprisonment for a term not exceeding six months or to a fine not exceeding the statutory maximum, or to both;

    b. on conviction on indictment, to imprisonment for a term not exceeding two years or to a fine of any amount, or to both.

4. No proceedings may be instituted for an offence relating to the ill-treatment of patients except by or with the consent of the Director of Public Prosecutions.

SEXUAL OFFENCES WITH THE SEVERELY MENTALLY HANDICAPPED

The Sexual Offences Act 1956, as amended by the Mental Health (Amendment) Act provides:

    1. It is an offence for a man to have unlawful sexual intercourse with a woman who is severely mentally handicapped (a

defective). This applies to any such woman whether in hospital or outside it.

2. A man is not guilty of an offence because he has unlawful sexual intercourse with a woman, if he does not know, and has no reason to suspect her to be severely mentally handicapped (a defective).

3. In this section 'severe mental handicap' means a state of arrested or incomplete development of mind which includes severe impairment of intelligence and social functioning.

Sexual intercourse with patients

1. It is an offence for a man who is an officer on the staff of a hospital or mental nursing home, or is otherwise employed there or who is one of the managers, to have unlawful sexual intercourse with a woman who is receiving psychiatric treatment in the hospital.

2. It is an offence for a male staff member to have unlawful sexual intercourse on the hospital premises with a woman who is receiving treatment there as an out-patient.

3. It is an offence for a man to have unlawful sexual intercourse with a woman mentally disordered patient who is subject to his guardianship. It is similarly an offence if the woman is in his custody and care under the Mental Health Act or, as a result of arrangements made under the National Assistance Act 1948, or as a resident in a home for the mentally disordered under the Mental Health Act. (Previously known as Part III accommodation with reference to the 1959 Act).

4. It is *not* an offence if the man has no reason to know, or suspect, that the woman is a mentally disordered patient.

Sexual Offences with a Male patient.

The Sexual Offences Act 1967 (Section 1) provides that it is an offence for a man to commit buggery or an act of gross indecency with another man, knowing him to be a severely mentally handicapped patient in hospital (or an out -patient). Although the 1967 Act provides that a severely handicapped patient cannot give consent, if the accused did not know, or suspect, that the patient was severely mentally handicapped he will not be guilty of an offence.

Penalties

Any person guilty of the offences described above involving female or male patients, or severely handicapped persons, is liable on conviction on indictment to imprisonment for a term not exceeding two years. No proceedings may be instituted except by, or with the consent of, the Director of Public Prosecutions.

ASSISTING PATIENTS TO BE ABSENT WITHOUT LEAVE (Section 128)

1. It is an offence to induce or knowingly assist a detained patient or a patient subject to guardianship to be absent without leave.

2. It is similarly an offence to assist any person who is in legal custody to escape.

3. Any person who knowingly harbours a patient who is absent without leave and liable to be brought back to hospital may be guilty of an offence. It is also an offence to give assistance with intent to prevent, hinder or interfere with his being taken into custody or being returned to hospital.

4. The penalties for this group of offences may be

   a. on summary conviction, to imprisonment for a term not exceeding six months, or to a fine not exceeding the statutory maximum, or both;
   b. on conviction of indictment to imprisonment for a term not exceeding two years or to a fine of any amount or both.

Obstruction (Section 129)

1. It is an offence to obstruct any person who is authorised to visit, interview or examine a patient, or inspect buildings or records. It is an offence to refuse to produce records or documents for inspection by an authorised person. It is an offence to refuse to leave when requested to do so by a person who is authorised to interview a patient in private.

2. These offences may lead on summary conviction to imprisonment for a term not exceeding three months or to a fine not exceeding level four on the standard scale, or both.

LEGAL PROTECTION OF STAFF (Section 139)

1. No person is liable to any civil or criminal proceedings in carrying out duties under the Act, unless the action was done in bad faith or without reasonable care.

2. No civil proceedings may be brought against any person in any court in respect of any such act without the leave of the High Court.

3. No criminal proceedings may be brought against any person in any court in respect of any such act except by or with the consent of the Director of Public Prosecutions.

4. The above does not apply in respect of an offence under any other provision of the Act which provides that the proceedings can *only* be instituted by or with the consent of the Director of Public Prosecutions.

5. The provisions in this Section of the Act do not apply to proceedings against the Secretary of State or against a health authority within the meaning of the National Health Service Act 1977. For such proceedings the consent of the High Court or the Director of Public Prosecutions is not required.

6. References to the Director of Public Prosecutions above shall be construed in relation to Northern Ireland as a reference to the Director of Public Prosecutions of Northern Ireland.

23 Duties of hospital managers

BACKGROUND

For National Health Service hospitals 'the managers' are members of a Regional Health Authority, a District Health Authority or members of a Board of Governors, or of a Special Health Authority. The management of Special Hospitals is vested in the Secretary of State. The power to detain a patient under the Act rests with the managers who receive the application made by the patient's nearest relative or an approved social worker, supported by appropriate medical recommendations. Although the managers have the ultimate responsibility for ensuring that their power to detain a patient is based upon an acceptable application, they are empowered to delegate the function of scrutinising documents and accepting the patient to administrative officers. In the past, this has sometimes become a routine chore, often carried out by relatively junior members of the administrative staff. It is, however, a responsible and important task, since it endorses the restriction of the liberty of a patient, and it is necessary for managers to ensure that an experienced person is entrusted with it. It is likely that the Mental Health Act Commission will monitor the way in which applications for detention are made and accepted in the future and patients will, of course, have many more opportunities to appeal to a Tribunal.

Some responsibilities of the managers, in particular the power to discharge a patient, may be carried out only by members of the management themselves and the Act allows three or more members to exercise this function, which may not be delegated to officers.

In relation to a mental nursing home, registered as required by the Nursing Homes Act 1975, 'the managers' are the person or persons in whose name the mental nursing home is registered.

PRINCIPAL CHANGES

1. The Mental Health Act 1983 places a duty upon managers to give information to detained patients as soon as possible after the patient has been admitted.

2. The managers have a further duty to inform the nearest relative when a detained patient has been discharged.

Duties of managers to give information

1. Section 132 requires the managers of a hospital or mental nursing home in which a patient is detained to take such steps as are practicable to ensure that the patient understands:

   a. under which of the provisions of the Act he is detained and its effects;
   b. his rights to apply to a Mental Health Review Tribunal.

2. These steps should be taken as soon as practicable after the commencement of the patient's detention under the Act and must take into account any cultural or language problems or other difficulties in communication.

3. The managers are also required to take such steps as are practicable to ensure that the patient understands the effect of

   a. discharge by the Responsible Medical Officer;
   b. discharge by the managers; or
   c. discharge by the nearest relative (and the restrictions on the nearest relatives power of discharge).

in so far as this information is relevant to his case.

4. The managers must, similarly, ensure that the patient understands the effect of the 'consent to treatment' requirements under the Act and the requirements of the Act with respect to patient's correspondence, the Code of Practice and the Mental Health Act Commission, in so far as this information is relevant to him and the Section of the Act under which he is detained.

5. As previously, this information should be given to the patient as soon as it is practicable after the commencement of his detention.

6. The managers must also, except where the patient requests that it is not done, furnish the nearest relative with a copy of any information given to the patient (as above). This information must be provided in writing and at the time the patient is informed or as soon as possible afterwards.

Duty of managers to inform nearest relative

1. In addition to other requirements in the Act for managers to give relatives information, when a patient (who is liable to be detained) is to be discharged, the nearest relative must be informed by the managers as soon as possible. If practicable this information should be given at least seven days before the discharge date.

2. This step is not required if the discharge is taking place as a result of an order made by the nearest relative.

3. The information that a patient is to be discharged should not be given to the nearest relative if the patient or his nearest relative has requested that it is not to be given.

Automatic referral of cases to a Tribunal

As described above (p. 96) the managers are required by the Act to refer certain cases to a Mental Health Review Tribunal at intervals.

24 Patient's correspondence (Section 134)

BACKGROUND

The Percy Commission recommended that there should not be any censorship of outgoing letters from any patient (whether detained or not) except at the request of individual addressees. They also expected that incoming mail would only be withheld in exceptional circumstances. Despite this, the powers to control mail provided in the 1959 Act were much wider and gave the Responsible Medical Officer authority to intercept mail if it would cause the patient unnecessary distress or interfere with his treatment. Outgoing mail could also be withheld at the request of individuals who might receive correspondence. These powers extended to informal patients for whom authority was vested in the doctor in charge of the patient's case and to patients under guardianship, but mail addressed to certain listed individuals such as Members of Parliament was exempt from any control.

These controls were generally thought to be much too restrictive and in the context of open wards with easy access to telephones and other forms of communication they were often impracticable. The staff often found the requirements unclear and this put an unreasonable burden or responsibility upon them.

The law in relation to patients' correspondence has, therefore, been revised but with particular concern for the problems of security that mainly affect the special hospitals. Patients must, for example, be prevented from being sent anything which might assist them to leave the hospital or might be used to attack others. This section of the Act (Section 134) completely replaces the law contained in the 1959 Act relating to correspondence.

Withholding out-going correspondence

1. Correspondence (a postal packet) addressed *by a detained* patient to a person outside the hospital may be withheld from the Post Office:

   a. If the person has requested that communications addressed to him by the patient should be withheld.
   b. If the hospital is a Special Hospital and the managers consider that the postal packet is likely:

i. to cause distress to the person to whom it is addressed or to any other person (not on the staff or the hospital);
ii. to cause danger to any person.

2. A person who wishes to request that communications are not sent to him is required to give notice in writing to the managers of the hospital, the doctor in charge of the patient's treatment, or the Secretary of State.

Withholding in-coming correspondence

1. A postal packet addressed *to a detained patient in a special hospital* may be withheld from the patient if, in the opinion of the managers of the hospital, it is necessary to do so:

i. in the interests of the safety of the patient; or
ii. for the protection of other persons.

Exceptions

Postal packets to or from the following may not be withheld (unless the person has specifically requested that communications addressed to him by the patient should be withheld):

a. Any Minister of the Crown or Member of either House of Parliament;
b. The Master or any other officer of the Court of Protection or any of the Lord Chancellor's Visitors;
c. the Parliamentary Commissioner for Administration, the Health Service Commissioner for England, the Health Service Commissioner for Wales or a Local Commissioner within the meaning of Part III of the Local Government Act 1974;
d. a Mental Health Review Tribunal;
e. A Health Authority within the meaning of the National Health Service Act 1977, a local Social Services Authority, a Community Health Council or a Probation and After-Care Committee;
f. The managers of the hospital in which the patient is detained;
g. Any legally qualified person instructed by the patient;
h. the European Commission of Human Rights or the European Court of Human Rights.

Administration

1. The managers of the hospital are empowered to inspect and open any postal packet to determine whether or not it should be withheld, or the contents should be withheld in accordance with the provisions described above.

2. When any correspondence is withheld the managers of the hospital should make a record in writing.

3. Where anything is withheld the managers must give notice of the fact to the patient *within seven days.* If the correspondence is addressed by a person to a patient in a Special Hospital the person must be notified in writing.

4. Notifications to the patient or person sending a communication to a patient in a Special Hospital must be accompanied by a statement

informing either of them of their rights of application to the Mental Health Act Commission (as follows):

5. The Commission must review any decision to withhold a postal packet (or its contents) if an application is made to them to do so (Section 121):

  a. by the patient;
  b. in the case of a Special Hospital patient to whom a postal packet has been addressed, by the patient or the person who sent it.
  Any application must be made within six months of being notified that the postal packet has been withheld.

6. The managers may delegate their functions in relation to correspondence to a person or persons on the staff of the hospital.

7. The Secretary of State may make Regulations with respect to his powers in relation to correspondence, setting out procedure for examining mail, the records to be kept, etc.

Informal or voluntary patients
None of the restrictions in connection with patient's correspondence applies to informal patients.

Mental Health Act Commission and Correspondence
Where an application has been made to the Commission to review a decision to withhold correspondence, the Commission may direct that it is not longer withheld from delivery. The Secretary of State may make Regulations providing for the production of any postal packet for inspection by the Commission.

REFERENCE
Mental Health (Hospital, Guardianship and Consent to Treatment) Regulations 1983

25 Removing patients to a 'place of safety'; retaking patients, removing patients in need of care

BACKGROUND

Infrequently, a family doctor, social worker, the police or other responsible person receives information that an apparently mentally disordered individual living alone is not able to care for himself properly and may be suffering as a result. Sometimes there is evidence of neglect or ill-treatment, or the patient may have withdrawn from the outside world, influenced by paranoid delusions or hallucinations.

The Act gives authority, on the warrant of a Justice of the Peace, for a police constable accompanied by a doctor and another person to enter premises and remove a patient to a place of safety for 72 hours. This gives time for decisions to be made and for the patient to be detained under another Section of the Act if this is necessary. This power has been used on an average number of nine occasions annually in England and Wales since 1974.

WARRANT TO SEARCH FOR AND REMOVE PATIENTS (SECTION 135)

1. Information must be provided on oath by a Mental Welfare Officer to a Justice of the Peace. If it appears that there is reasonable reason to suspect that a person believed to be suffering from mental disorder:

   a. has been, or is being, ill-treated, neglected or kept otherwise than under proper control (in any place within the Justice's jurisdiction;) or
   b. is a person who is unable to care for himself and is living alone

then the Justice may issue a warrant. This provides authorisation for a police constable to enter premises by force if necessary. If it is thought fit, the patient may be removed to a place of safety with a view to detaining him under another Section of the Act, or to making other arrangements for his treatment or care.

2. A patient may be detained under this Section for a period not exceeding 72 hours.

3. In executing the warrant the police constable must be accompanied by a Mental Welfare Officer and by a medical practitioner.

4. The patient shall not be named in any information or warrant.

RETAKING A PATIENT (SECTION 135(2))

1. Any constable, or other person authorised by or under the Act to take a patient to any place, take a patient into custody, or retake a patient (who is liable to be retaken) may lay information before a Justice of the Peace on oath.

2. The Justice of the Peace may issue a warrant authorising any named police constable to enter the premises, by force if necessary, to remove the patient.

3. The *grounds* for issuing such a warrant are:

    a. that there is reasonable cause to believe that the patient is to be found on the premises within the Justice's jurisdiction; and

    b. that admission to the premises has been refused, or that the patient has indicated his refusal to admit anyone.

4. In executing the warrant the police constable may be accompanied by

    a. a medical practitioner;

    b. any person authorised under the Act (or the Scotland Act) to take or retake the patient.

MENTALLY DISORDERED PERSONS FOUND IN PUBLIC PLACES

1. The Act authorises a police constable who finds a *person who appears to be suffering from mental disorder*, in a place to which the public has access, to remove him to a place of safety. He may do so if the person

    a. appears to be in immediate need of care and control;

    b. if the police constable thinks that it is necessary to do so in the person's interests or for the protection of other persons.

2. A person removed to a place of safety from a public place may be detained in a place of safety for a period not exceeding 72 hours. This is for the purpose of enabling the patient to be examined by a registered medical practitioner and to be interviewed by an Approved Social Worker, and for the purpose of making any necessary arrangements for his treatment and care.

In 1979 the police removed 1623 persons to a hospital (as a 'place of safety') for examination. An unknown number of people were taken to a police station, since no record is kept of the use of a police station as a 'place of safety'. However, researchers have commented that, in so far as hospital cases are concerned, the police appear to have used their powers under this Section responsibly, but it has been *suggested* that an improved records system should be introduced in the future and Chief Constables should be required to record when a police station has been used as a 'place of safety'.

Place of safety
A 'place of safety' referred to in the above Sections of the Act means

a. residential accommodation provided by a local authority under Part III of the National Assistance Act 1948, or under Paragraph 2, Schedule 8 of the National Health Service Act 1977;
b. a hospital as defined by this Act;
c. a police station;
d. a mental nursing home or residential home for mentally disordered persons; or
e. any other suitable place, the occupier of which is willing temporarily to receive the patient.

Custody, conveyance and detention (Section 137)
1. Section 42(6) (Powers of Secretary of State in respect of restricted patients) authorises the Secretary of State to direct a patient who is subject to a restriction order to attend at any place for the purpose of any public inquiry or the interests of justice. He may then require the patient to be kept in custody while being taken there and back. He is then deemed to be *in legal custody* (Section 137).

2. Similarly, a constable or other authorised person permitted by the Act to take a person into custody, convey or detain him is provided (Section 137(2)) with 'all the powers, authorities, protection and privileges which a constable has within the area for which he acts as constable'.

RETAKING PATIENTS ESCAPING FROM CUSTODY

1. If any person in legal custody escapes he may be retaken

a. by the person who had custody immediately before the escape, or by any constable or Approved Social Worker.
b. If liable to be detained under Part II of the Act at the time of the escape (or subject to guardianship), he may be retaken by any other person who could take him into custody if he had absented himself without leave (see Chapter 35).

2. A person subject to detention on a Hospital Order under Part II of the Act (or subject to guardianship) may not be retaken after expiration of the period, which limits retaking him if he is absent without leave and fails to return (unless he is on a restriction order).

3. Similarly a patient who is being detained under Section 135 or 136 cannot be retaken after 72 hours beginning with the time that he escapes or the period during which he is liable to be detained, whichever expires first.

26 Miscellaneous matters

EXAMINATION OF MEMBERS OF PARLIAMENT (SECTION 141)

Background

The 1983 Act, like its predecessor, makes special provision for the examination of a Member of Parliament who is detained under a Section of the Act, since he will be unable to represent his constituents and, if detained for a lengthy period, he may be required to vacate his seat. The 1959 Act required the Speaker to request (in England and Wales or Northern Ireland) the President of the Royal College of Physicians of London, or (for Members of Parliament taken ill in Scotland) the President of the Royal College of Physicians of Edinburgh and the President of the Royal Faculty of Physicians and Surgeons of Glasgow acting jointly, to nominate two doctors to examine the Member and to make a report.

Principle change

The arrangements are amended so that the Speaker is now required to ask the *President of the Royal College of Psychiatrists* to nominate the two doctors.

Requirements

1. Where a Member of the House of Commons is detained on the ground that he is suffering from *mental illness* it is the duty of the court, authority or person on whose order or application the detention was authorised to notify the Speaker of the House of Commons that the Member has been detained. A medical practitioner who makes a recommendation and the person in charge of the hospital (or other place) in which the Member is detained must similarly inform the Speaker.

2. If the Speaker is informed as above, or is notified by two members of the House of Commons that they are 'credibly informed' that such a notification has been given, then he shall require him to be examined by two registered medical practitioners appointed by the President of the Royal College of Psychiatrists, being practitioners appearing to the President to have special experience in the diagnosis or treatment of mental disorders.

3. The medical practitioners shall report to the Speaker with their opinion as to whether the Member is suffering from mental illness and is authorised to be detained for that reason.

4. If the Member is suffering from mental illness he must be revisited in a further six months. If his illness and detention continues the Speaker must lay both doctors' reports before the House of Commons and the seat of the Member shall thereupon become vacant.

VOTING RIGHTS OF PATIENTS

Background
Previously the Representation of the People Act 1959 barred all patients in mental hospitals from exercising their right to vote, even though they may be informal and competent patients. For some patients the hospital is, in effect, their home but they were unable to be registered or to vote.

Principal change
From 1st April 1983 informal patients in mental hospitals will be able to make a declaration which allows their names to be included in the electoral register. This results from Section 62 of the Mental Health (Amendment) Act which amended the Representation of the People Act 1949. The procedure required in order that the patient may make a legal and valid declaration is laid down in Schedule 2 of the Mental Health (Amendment) Act and Health Authorities were notified of the new provisions in a circular issued by the DHSS in 1983. These arrangements are now consolidated in the Representation of the People Act 1983.

POCKET MONEY (SECTION 122)

The Act authorises the Secretary of State to pay such amounts as he thinks fit in respect of occasional personal expenses to patients receiving in-patient treatment in hospital. This applies to all patients, detained or informal, and applies to in-patients in Special Hospitals and other hospitals, wholly or mainly used for the treatment of persons suffering from mental disorder. The arrangements similarly apply to patients for whom hospital services are provided under the National Health Service Act 1977.

Section 142 describes arrangements for directing periodic payments arising from any pension or other fund to an institution or person having care of a patient if, on medical evidence, the patient is considered incapable of managing his property and affairs as a consequence of mental disorder.

REFERENCE
Health circular 1983 Electoral registration in mental illness and mental handicap hospitals. DHSS. London

Glossary

Absent without leave	Absent from any hospital or other place and liable to be taken into custody and returned under Section 18.
Appropriate Medical Officer	a. For patients subject to guardianship of a person (not the local social services authority) the Nominated Medical Attendant. b. In any other case, the Responsible Medical Officer.
Approved Doctor	A registered medical practitioner approved for purposes of Section 12 by the Secretary of State as having special experience in the diagnosis or treatment of mental disorder.
Approved Social Worker	An officer of a local social services authority appointed to act as an Approved Social Worker for the purposes of the Act.
Hospital	a. Any health service hospital within the meaning of the National Health Service Act 1977. b. Any accommodation provided by a local authority and used as a hospital by or on behalf of the Secretary of State under the National Health Service Act 1977.
Hospital Order	Order for the admission of an offender to hospital.
Local social services authority	A council which is a local authority for the purpose of the Local Authority Social Services Act 1970.
Managers, the	a. In relation to a hospital vested in the Secretary of State for the purposes of his function under the National Health Service Act 1977, and in relation to any accommodation provided by a local authority

and used as a hospital by or on behalf of the Secretary of State under that Act: the District Health Authority or special health authority responsible for the administration of the hospital.

b. In relation to a Special Hospital the Secretary of State.

c. In relation to a mental nursing home registered under the Nursing Homes Act 1975, the person or persons registered in respect of the home.

Medical treatment

Includes nursing, and also includes care, habilitation and rehabilitation under medical supervision.

Nominated Medical Attendant

A registered medical practitioner appointed to act as 'appropriate medical officer' to a patient subject to the guardianship of a person (not the local social services authority).

Patient

Except in relation to the Court of Protection, patient means a person suffering or appearing to be suffering from mental disorder.

Responsible Medical Officer

a. In relation to a patient liable to be detained in hospital for assessment or treatment, the registered medical practitioner in charge of the treatment of the patient.

b. In relation to a patient subject to guardianship, the medical officer authorised by the local social services authority to act (either generally or in any particular case or for any particular purpose) as the Responsible Medical Officer.

Restricted patient

A patient who is subject to a restriction order or a restriction direction.

Appendix

ADDRESSES

REGIONAL TRIBUNAL OFFICES:

Mental Health Review Tribunals
Hepburn House
Marsham Street
London SW1P 4HW

Tel: 01-211-7325
     01-211-7356

Mental Health Review Tribunals
3rd floor
Cressington House
249 St. Mary's Road
Garston
Liverpool
L19 0NF

Tel: 051-494-0095

Mental Health Review Tribunals
Spur A, Block 5
Government Buildings
Chalfont Drive
Western Boulevard
Nottingham NG8 3RZ

Tel: 0602-294222/3

Mental Health Review Tribunals
2nd Floor
New Crown Buildings
Cathays Park
Cardiff CF1 3NQ

Tel: 0222-825798

DEPARTMENT OF HEALTH & SOCIAL SECURITY

Mental Health Division
Alexander Fleming House
Elephant & Castle
London SE1 6BY

Tel: 01-407-5522

MENTAL HEALTH ACT COMMISSION

(Regional Offices)

1. (London Office)
   floors 1 and 2
   Hepburn House
   Marsham Street
   London
   SW1P 4HW
   Tel: 01-211-8061
        01-211-4337

2. (Liverpool Office)
   Cressington House
   249 St. Mary's Road
   Garston
   Liverpool
   L19 0NF
   Tel: 051-427-2061
        051-427-6213

3. (Nottingham Office)
   Spur A, Block 5
   Government Buildings
   Chalfont Drive
   Western Boulevard
   Nottingham NG8 3R2
   Tel: 0602-293409
        0602-293198

COURT OF PROTECTION

Chief Clerk
Court of Protection
Staffordshire House
25 Store Street
London WC1E 7BP

Tel: 01-636-6877

C3 DIVISION, HOME OFFICE

C3 Division
Home Office
50 Queen Anne's Gate
London SW1H 9AT

Tel: 01-213-7355

LAW SOCIETY – LEGAL AID AREA CENTRES ENGLAND AND WALES

No. 1 London South

The Law Society
No 1 Legal Aid Area
Area Headquarters
29/37 Red Lion Street
London WC1R 4PP

Tel: 01-405-6991

No. 2 South-Eastern

The Law Society
No. 2 Legal Aid Area
Area Headquarters
9-12 Middle Street
Brighton BN1 1AS

Tel: 0273-27003

No. 3 Southern

The Law Society
No. 3 Legal Aid Area
Area Headquarters
Crown House
10 Crown Street
Reading RG1 2SJ

Tel: 0734-589696

No. 4 South-Western

The Law Society
No. 4 Legal Aid Area
Area Headquarters
Whitefriars (Block 'C')
Lewins Mead
Bristol BS1 2LR

Tel: 0272-214801

No. 5 South Wales

The Law Society
No. 5 Legal Aid Area
Area Headquarters
Marland House
Central Square
Cardiff CF1 1PF

Tel: 0222 388971/7

No. 6 West-Midland

The Law Society
No. 6 Legal Aid Area
Area Headquarters
Podium
Centre City House
5 Hill Street
Birmingham B5 4UD

Tel: 021-632-6541

No. 7 North Western

The Law Society
No. 7 Legal Aid Area
Area Headquarters
Pall Mall Court
67 King Street
Manchester M60 9AX

Tel: 061-832-7112

No. 8 Northern

The Law Society
No. 8 Legal Aid Area
Area Headquarters
18 Newgate Shopping Centre
Newcastle Upon Tyne
NE1 5RU

Tel: 0632 23461/4

No. 9 North Eastern

The Law Society
No. 9 Legal Aid Area
Area Headquarters
City House
New Station Street
Leeds LS1 4JS

Tel: 0532 442851/6

No. 10 East Midland

The Law Society
No. 10 Legal Aid Area
Area Headquarters
5 Friar Lane
Nottingham NG1 6BW

Tel: 0602 42341/4

No. 11 Eastern

The Law Society
No. 11 Legal Aid Area
Area Headquarters
Kett House
Station Road
Cambridge CB1 2JT

Tel: 0223 66511/7

No. 12 Chester and District
The Law Society
No. 12 Legal Aid Area
Area Headquarters
North West House
City Road
Chester CH1 2AL

Tel: 0244-23591

No. 13 London East

The Law Society
No. 13 Legal Aid Area
Area Headquarters
29/37 Red Lion Street
London WC1R 4PP

Tel: 01-405 6991

No. 14 London West

The Law Society
No 14 Legal Aid Area
Area Headquarters
29/37 Red Lion Street
London WC1R 4PP

Tel: 01-405-6991

No. 15 Merseyside

The Law Society
No. 15 Legal Aid Area
Area Headquarters
Moor House
James Street
Liverpool L2 7SA

Tel: 051-236-8371

Index